HOW TO MAKE LUCK

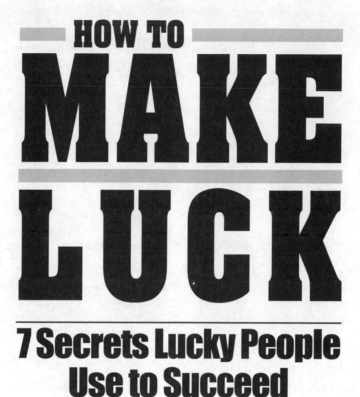

HOW TO
MAKE
LUCK

7 Secrets Lucky People Use to Succeed

MARC MYERS

RENAISSANCE BOOKS
Los Angeles

For Alyse and Olivia,
the loves of my life

Copyright © 1999 by Marc Myers

Library of Congress Cataloging-in-Publication Data
Myers, Marc.
    How to make luck : the seven secrets lucky people use to succeed /
Marc Myers.
       p. cm.
    ISBN 1-58063-058-8 (pbk. : alk. paper)
    1. Success—Psychological aspects. 2. Fortune. I. Title.
BF637.S8M94 1999
158.1—dc21   98-47882
                                                             CIP

10 9 8 7 6 5 4 3 2 1
Design by Susan Shankin

Distributed by St. Martin's Press
Manufactured in the United States of America
First Edition

Contents

Part Three: How to Limit Bad Luck 177

Acknowledgments

When my agent first suggested I write a book about luck and how anyone could become luckier, I said I wasn't sure I was qualified.

I wasn't a lottery winner, a movie star, or a real estate developer. But my agent cut me off. "Are you kidding?" she said. "It doesn't matter. You're the luckiest person I know. Think about it—and think about all the lucky people you know." And the more I thought about it, the more I realized she was right. If being lucky is about being incredibly fortunate and happy, I certainly was lucky.

I told my agent I'd think about it. About half an hour later I was walking up New York's Seventh Avenue, near Carnegie Hall, when I looked down. There on the sidewalk was a dollar bill stop-starting its way toward me. A final gust of autumn wind sent the bill up against the leg of my jeans. It was when I bent down to pick up the bill that I decided to write this book. I'm not particularly superstitious, but I can take a hint.

Much of my good luck owes a great deal to the many people who graciously helped me with advice, friendship, and support during this project. I'd like to thank them here.

First, my wife, Alyse, and daughter, Olivia, my guardian angels. More about them later.

Joe McNeely, Renaissance Media's director of acquisitions, who understood from the beginning the purpose and power of what I wanted to say and became the book's biggest champion.

Laura Golden Bellotti, my Los Angeles editor at Renaissance Books, who wriggled inside my manuscript and provided masterful guidance. I was very lucky to work with Laura. Every writer should be so fortunate.

Ann Hartley, a meticulous copy editor and consummate professional.

Marty Edelston, whose generosity, strength, and wisdom have been invaluable. I am truly lucky to know him.

Sheree Bykofsky, my literary agent on this project, who lit the fuse and convinced me to share my lucky secrets.

The powerful and shrewd Kate White, editor-in-chief of *Cosmopolitan*, who started me thinking about this project before it ever came up. You were on my mind during all of those late nights when I didn't think I had the energy to write another sentence.

The great Stephen Covey, whose perspective on human behavior and life is truly amazing.

Lee Riffaterre and Marty Shenkman, two of the wisest attorneys I know.

Fund manager Jim O'Shaugnessy, whose hard-charging energy level and high-octane spirit kept me supercharged.

Money maven Michael Stolper, whose vision, honesty, and intellect were awesome.

Hollywood publicist Michael Levine, who believed in me and this project early on and helped me envision the finished product.

The brilliant and gentle Adam Robinson, who could always be counted on for his enthusiasm and feedback.

Laura Day, whose radiance and energy were inspiring.

Jeri Sedlar, for all of her sunshine and support.

All of the people who shared with me their stories but made me promise not to use their names in this book. You know who you are and why you're so special to me.

My mother, Bernice Myers, the children's book writer and illustrator, who taught me about unconditional optimism and to always tell the truth.

My father, Lou Myers, the great cartoonist, writer, and humorist, who taught me why it pays to be aggressive, industrious, and inflexible about deadlines.

Lisa, David, and Matthew, whose warmth and encouragement made all the difference.

Artist Nelson Diaz, whose friendship and spiritual insights, and our mutual love of jazz, made our Saturday morning get-togethers in his SoHo studio real eye-openers and helped me see luck from many angles.

All of the great people at Boardroom Inc., whose efficiency and professionalism during the day allowed me to devote my nights and weekends to writing this book.

All of my freelance writers at *Bottom Line/Personal* and *Moneysworth* who cheered me on.

Finally, two people without whom this book would not have been possible:

Alyse, my amazing, beautiful, and brilliant wife, whose emotional support and magical powers have made all of my dreams come true. I was lucky to have met you.

And Olivia, my darling nine-year-old daughter, whose mischievous sense of humor, understanding, and surprise-attack kisses kept me going. Yes, Olivia, I'm finally finished with my book.

Introduction

Admit it. You're reading this book because you've always been a little curious about lucky people. How do they manage to lead such charmed lives? How are they able to get so much of what they want without appearing to work too hard to get it? Is their repeated good fortune the gift of chance? A matter of superb timing? A lot of hard work? Or are they simply blessed?

I wrote this book to let you in on a simple yet life-changing secret: The people we think of as lucky merely behave in ways that are so special and seductive that nearly everyone they meet feels compelled to offer them great opportunities. It is this wealth of opportunities that allows them to continuously improve their good luck. If you want to be lucky too, all you have to do is start behaving lucky.

I have always been fascinated by people who regularly get what they want. But I've never fully believed that lucky people are magical recipients of good fortune while the rest of us must work hard and long to achieve success. First of all, hard work—by itself—doesn't guarantee that you'll get what you want or that you'll get it anytime soon. And secondly, I've carefully observed lucky people long enough to know that although some of them work hard, their true key to success is knowing how to encourage others to help them and offer them great opportunities.

Before you begin to read this book, your first step to becoming lucky is to realize that there is a big difference between luck and chance. Chance is what happens when you interact with the random world around you. Every time you walk outside, you encounter unexpected events. Anything can happen. You may find $100 on the sidewalk—or a safe might hit you on the head. Such experiences are random, and there isn't much you can do to predict or prepare for them. Stuff happens, and that's life.

Luck is different. Your luck depends on the actions of other people and whether or not they decide to help you get what you want. The faster you identify the people who can make your life easier, and the more skillful you are at convincing them you're worth helping, the luckier you will be.

While most of us are convinced that luck is something we do not have control over, we nonetheless continue to be obsessed with it. Frustrated by the slow pace of hard work and intrigued by the possibility of becoming instantly rich, we grow impatient waiting for our ships to come in. Fueling our imaginations is the endless parade of people who seem to have gotten what they want without having done much to get it. You can't open a magazine or newspaper or turn on the television today without seeing a story about someone who was amazingly fortunate. But the more credit we give chance for such occurrences, the less likely we are to realize that we each have the ability to make good luck happen—and that it's not so hard!

In this book, I will show you specific steps you can take to attract more good luck and to limit your bad luck. All you need to do to become lucky is get better at creating opportunities and limiting calamities. While most of us will never win a lottery or become a CEO, we can become luckier than we are now—without overworking or standing around waiting for fortune to smile on us.

In part one, I will show you that luck and success are inextricably linked, that one is not possible without the other. The reason most people don't spend more time trying to improve their luck is that they don't think there's much they can do about it. That's one of a number of "good luck myths" that I'll talk about in this part of the book. You'll also learn that you are a lot luckier than you think, and that by getting into some very simple lucky habits, life will become more rewarding.

In part two, I'll explore why most of the people whom you think of as lucky aren't any more or less blessed by chance than you are. They are just extremely proficient at one or more of seven behavior skills necessary to make life go their way. You only have to improve your ability in one or more of these seven areas to improve your own luck.

Being lucky is also about minimizing your bad luck, and you will learn in part three the strategies that lucky people use to keep misfortune from undermining their efforts to succeed.

Mastering these lucky skills won't guarantee that you'll instantly have it all. But you will find yourself easily attracting the opportunities and advantages that will help you achieve your wildest dreams. You'll also realize you've become one of the luckiest people around.

PART ONE

DEVELOPING A GOOD-LUCK PERSONALITY

Throw a lucky man into the sea and
he will come out with a fish in his mouth.

UNKNOWN

Short of breaking the law, there seem to be just two ways to get what you want in life. You can work hard and maybe your efforts will pay off. Or you can wish for what you want and hope it will land in your lap. Most people use one strategy or the other—or a combination of the two—to make their dreams come true. Unfortunately, the odds of realizing your fantasies using these two strategies aren't very good.

The problem with hard work is that it doesn't guarantee success— nor does it guarantee that success will come as quickly as you'd like. We all know people who work seventy-hour weeks and never achieve what they want. Hard work just isn't very efficient. It's time consuming. You have to juggle dozens of tasks, anticipate problems, make decisions, undo some of those decisions, and learn from your mistakes. Yet there's no telling whether all of the time and energy spent will produce your desired results.

Hard work can even work against you. We've all thrown ourselves into projects with hopes of achieving goals but later found that we had worked too hard on the wrong things. In other cases, our tireless efforts went unnoticed or were unappreciated.

When hard work fails to make dreams come true—as is often the case—frustration sets in. The truth is that hard work doesn't get us what we want nearly as often as most people think.

When hard work fails to produce the desired results and discouragement sets in, many people give up on striving to reach their goals and instead use the second strategy—*wishing* for the things they want. Just look at the jump in lottery-ticket sales, the boom in casino gambling, and the stock market's popularity. All hold out the promise that anyone can get what they want without having to do much to get it. Just the term "instant millionaire" is enough to send our imaginations racing off to Ferrari dealerships and real estate agents. We are excited by accelerated success, especially the kind that takes very little apparent effort, and we want to believe such miracles can happen to us. Maybe that's the real reason why movies with plots based on love at first sight are so popular. Eyes meet, hearts beat, and love catches fire—no endless hours in front of the phone waiting for it to ring, no getting up the courage to ask someone out, no bad conversations, hurt feelings, or bad hair days. Just instant happiness.

The problem with wishing for overnight success or instant rewards is that the odds of amazing good fortune arriving unexpectedly are about a million to one. So if you're hoping for good luck to transform your life, you probably will have to wait even longer than the people who are working really hard for their big payoff.

There is a *third* way to make your dreams come true: Behave and act lucky. Lucky people take very specific steps to improve their odds of good things happening to them. They also do things to limit their "bad luck." Like the rest of us, lucky people work hard and wish for good things to happen. What sets them apart, however, is what they do to attract opportunities, *to make luck happen to them*. Their attitudes and actions are so seductive and infectious that people line up to help these "lucky people" get what they want. Fortunately, most of the skills lucky people possess can be mastered by anyone. By adapting the frame of mind and the habits of people who always seem to get what they want, you can experience an enriched life and plenty of good fortune.

I am *not* suggesting that you manipulate people. I believe it's impossible to become lucky through trickery or deception. Once fooled, most people will go out of their way to seek revenge, which would certainly not enhance your good fortune. You become lucky by artfully exhibiting humility and character—allowing the attractiveness of your honesty, enthusiasm, and sincerity to compel others to help you achieve your goals.

■ CHAPTER ONE ■

Good Luck Is Something You Make

*Get as much experience as you can so that
you're ready when luck works.*

HENRY FONDA

The word *luck* dates back to the thirteenth century, when it entered the Middle Dutch language as *luk*. The *Oxford Dictionary of English Etymology* says the word probably began as a gambling term. But the word may owe more to the medieval town of Lucca, Italy, than to a wager won in a Flemish game of chance.

By the early 1200s, Italy had established itself as Europe's most exciting destination for ambitious traders. Ports on both of Italy's coasts had access to calm seas, and weather conditions were moderate year-round. Northern Italy's proximity to the rest of Europe and Asia exposed it to a wide range of cultures and ideas. Merchants from as far north as the Baltics, Holland, and England sailed down along the coast of France and around Spain to Italy's west coast port, Pisa. Traders from the Orient sailed into Venice on Italy's east coast.

During this period, Holland was the most powerful trading nation in Europe and its financial skills were unsurpassed. Dutch seafaring towns embarked on enormous commercial expansion in the thirteenth century, and Dutch sailors, traders, and fishermen routinely shuttled back and forth to Italy.

As trading picked up in the latter part of the thirteenth century, so did the demand for silver, which had begun to be mined on a large scale in Europe earlier in the century. Silver was much more efficient than barter and more plentiful in Europe than gold. Cities throughout Europe operated mines, and much of the mined silver was sent to mints in Pisa, Genoa, and Venice, where ingots were stamped into coins. During this period, a large percentage of the precious metal moved through Pisa, since it was easier for western European merchants to ship ingots for minting there, than it was to sail all the way around the boot of Italy to Venice.

Venice used a clever strategy to maintain its share of the silver market. To attract the silver that poured into the Pisa region, Venice decided in 1270 to kick off one of history's first tax breaks on shopping. It exempted the men of Lucca—a town twelve miles from Pisa—from having to pay the customary bullion tax on whatever ingots the men brought with them to purchase goods in Venice.

Given the close commercial relationship between Holland and Italy at this time, as well as the fact that Lucca's traders and bankers traveled all over Europe, *luk* may have been the word the Dutch traders used to describe the good fortune and tax-free status Lucca's men enjoyed.

Whatever *luck*'s origin, the word soon made its way across to England, where it turned up in Shakespeare's *Merry Wives of Windsor* in 1598 ("Good luck lies in odd numbers. . . . They say there is divinity in odd numbers, either in nativity, chance or death. . . ."), George

Meriton's *Yorkshire Dialogue* in 1683, and Jonathan Swift's *Polite Conversation* in 1738. How and when *luck,* the noun, became *lucky,* the adjective, is unknown. But the word *lucky* finds its way into print in the mid-nineteenth century—and almost always in relation to people with a knack for winning a gambling stake.

Today we've extended that definition. In an age when science has a logical explanation for almost everything, we use the words "luck" and "lucky" to help us rationalize anything that's incomprehensible. We call it luck when someone we know who isn't particularly attractive finds happiness with a handsome or beautiful lover, or when someone at work who doesn't seem very smart gets a promotion. People who survive train wrecks are lucky, as is the seemingly mediocre student who gets into an Ivy League school, or the young actress who lands her first role in a movie and wins an Oscar. Luck's existence is confirmed every time someone gets what he or she wants and makes that triumph look easy.

In other words, luck is used as a convenient explanation for any event that we don't want to believe was caused by another person's effort. When someone we know gets a big promotion or raise, or a friend tells us about a sexy person they met at a party, we call their good fortune *luck.* Attributing other people's good fortune to luck allows us to feel better about not getting what they got. Face it—if we were to admit that all of the great things that happen to others was the result of their effort and not serendipity, we would hate ourselves for not trying harder or not being smarter or not being more attractive.

So—the word *luck* has become an escape clause, a way to let ourselves off the hook. When we use it to describe another person's success or happiness, the word *luck* is a balm that soothes the sting of jealousy and guilt. And it comes to mean that which eludes us.

Does Luck Really Exist?

One of the luckiest days in history is said to have been June 6, 1944—D-Day—when allied troops took advantage of a break in the weather to invade Europe and eventually defeat the Nazis. Yet the decision to invade wasn't completely the result of fate and good luck.

As early as March 1942, General Dwight Eisenhower began contemplating an invasion of Nazi-occupied France. Tactical plans were prepared, spies tested the sands of French beaches, and arms, planes, ships, and men were amassed along the English Channel inlets. By late spring of 1944, Eisenhower knew that the large armada he had assembled had to strike soon or risk being detected by the Germans.

The target date for attack was set for early June. But the weather, which had been flawless during the first three days of the month, took a turn for the worse. By June 4, a drizzle became a cold, driving rain, transforming the English Channel into a rolling, violent sea. On June 5, as the rain beat against his window, Eisenhower was told by his staff that there was a good chance of a thirty-six-hour break in the storm during the early hours of June 6. Upon hearing that, Eisenhower gave the green light to invade. The storm did break as expected, and the rest is history.

Were Eisenhower's decision and success pure luck? Not exactly. While the break in the weather certainly was a stroke of good fortune, Eisenhower's decision to believe the weather forecast he was given wasn't based on superstition or military restlessness. Aware that military history was jammed with generals who mistakenly sent thousands of their men to death out of sheer frustration with the enemy or the weather, Eisenhower had taken steps to limit his chances of failure. Four weeks prior to the invasion, he met privately each day with Captain J. M. Stagg, a twenty-eight-year-old Scottish meteorologist. Stagg would bring Eisenhower the weather forecast and then remain for a half hour to answer dozens of Eisenhower's questions.

Eisenhower's biographer and D-Day author and historian, Stephen Ambrose, told me that Eisenhower went through this meticulous process to get a strong feel for Stagg's reasoning. Eisenhower wanted to have a clear sense of how Stagg made his predictions and how accurate they were. Eisenhower knew that the weather over southeast England, the English Channel, and France's Normandy region was unpredictable, and had anticipated that a successful invasion would depend on the accuracy of a forecast.

In effect, Eisenhower had taken careful, calculated steps to improve the odds of success and reduce his odds of failure. While Eisenhower's decision to invade may have seemed like a lucky call, he had actually taken a great deal of care to improve the odds of a favorable outcome. Had Eisenhower not sized up the accuracy of his weather forecaster, he may have doubted Stagg's prediction in light of the horrible weather at the time and delayed the invasion, giving up the critical element of surprise.

Like Eisenhower's unexpected and ill-timed torrential rains, many of the dilemmas and challenges we face start as uninvited random events. Each day, when you leave the house, you enter a random world. Some of the random events that surround you pass you by. Some collide with you. Some are within reach and must be grabbed or encouraged to come to you. How you deal with these random events determines your luck. Whenever you walk down the street, you have dozens of choices to make. You can walk right past everyone you meet. You can walk directly into them, which probably would result in an argument or a fight. Or you could stop and talk to every person you encounter, which could take all day, even if it did produce a number of interesting opportunities.

The point is, your behavior controls the quality of your luck. Act angry all of the time, and few people are going to want to befriend you or help you achieve your goals. Take steps to be more friendly, and you immediately have improved the odds of getting more of what you want, faster. We can control what we say and do. Everything else that happens to us depends on the actions of others and the random world in which we live. The only way to influence what we can't control is to take steps to attract the good things and deflect the bad.

Even inaction has an influence on our luck. Do nothing to get a raise, and the current value of your income will diminish over time. Say nothing at a party, and your odds of meeting someone special are close to zero. Tell no one that you want a promotion at work, and you leave your destiny in the hands of others. Your odds of success in such situations are always low, since such opportunities almost always go to those who ask or show interest.

The good news is that once you make specific changes in your behavior, you can attract more good luck. Experiencing good fortune depends on how skillful you are at influencing people to offer you opportunities and how well you manage those opportunities once they are offered.

Making the Switch from Wishing to Doing

I have always been conscious that luck depends on how well you influence events that appear out of your control. That's why I've always opted for doing rather than wishing.

Several years ago, my family was living in a one-bedroom co-op apartment in New York City. The place was claustrophobic and became even tighter when my daughter, Olivia, was born. We needed a larger place, but we couldn't find a buyer for our co-op. Just when we thought we were going to have to live in that apartment forever, a young couple showed up. They loved the place. We came to terms, but when the couple was interviewed by the building's co-op board, which decides who gets to move into the building and who does not, half the board didn't want to let the couple in. The couple wanted to put down just ten percent, rather than the customary twenty percent. So the co-op board decided it would discuss the matter and vote on it. I could have left the vote to chance, under the assumption that there was little I could do legally to influence their vote. But leaving my family's fate to chance—fifty-fifty odds—didn't seem smart. The downside was too devastating to consider.

So I wrote the board a letter. I respectfully and passionately explained that we were cramped in the apartment and that our potential buyers were the first we had seen in years. I also pointed out that the couple would be happy to take out insurance to guarantee that they wouldn't default on their mortgage or their maintenance payments. I also told the board that I didn't know whether my family could hold out much longer in such tight space. I delivered the letter and waited for the vote. I had tilted the table a little in my favor, treating the board members with respect and showing them how their biggest fears might be put to rest. The board approved the couple by one vote.

Everyone I know called me lucky at the time. And I suppose I was. But I hadn't left everything to chance. I had influenced my luck by taking steps to improve my odds of getting what I wanted. That experience taught me an important lesson. Ask yourself a simple question whenever you find yourself wishing for good luck: What can I do to influence the odds of my success? It also taught me to never under-estimate the power of a respectful, heartfelt letter.

If taking the right action improves our luck, why do so many people spend so much time wishing rather than doing? Because we give up hope and think that nothing we can do will have much of an impact on our circumstances. We wish for good luck when we feel helpless and need to get out of a jam. We also wish when we want something fast and don't believe there's anything we can do to get what we want quickly. We wish when we interview for a job. We wish when we make a pitch for new business. We wish all will go well when we must speak in front of an audience. In each of these instances, we hope that our wishes will be heard and that somehow we will be given just the edge we need to keep from failing.

But wishing doesn't make it so. The trick to truly improving your chances of success is to stop wishing and ask yourself what steps can be taken to make "good luck" happen to you.

> *Here are some initial questions to ask yourself.*
> *They will help you begin to switch from wishing to doing . . .*

- **What am I wishing for?**
- **Why am I wishing for it?**
- **Are there steps I could have taken so that I wouldn't be wishing now?**
- **What can I do now to improve the odds of getting what I'm wishing for?**
- **If the ideas in the previous question don't work out, what additional steps can I take to get another shot at what I want?**

You're Luckier Than You Think

People who believe they are unlucky spend their entire lives playing defense. They only take action when bad things happen to them. Then they frantically try to dig themselves out of whatever mess they are in. Once order has been restored to their lives, they then go back to being passive, choosing not to engage the many opportunities that slide past them. "Why bother?" they ask themselves.

The funny thing is that even people who don't think of themselves as fortunate are luckier than they think. This was shown in a recent study on luck done in England. The psychology professors at the University of Hertfordshire, near London, went out into the country-side and invited one hundred people to participate in an experiment. Half the participants claimed they were lucky while the other half claimed they were mostly unlucky. They were all brought to campus to take a computerized coin-toss test. Each person watched as a cartoon elf trotted across a computer screen and flipped a coin. Each was asked to call heads or tails.

When the results were added up, an amazing pattern emerged: The people who thought they were lucky had guessed right about the same amount of times as those who said they were unlucky. In the end, those who thought they were unlucky really weren't any more fortunate or unfortunate than those who insisted they were lucky. After conducting further interviews, the professors discovered that people who said they were lucky were more likely to remember the good things that happened to them over the course of their lives and forgot the bad things. The opposite was true for the self-proclaimed unlucky ones. They mostly recalled the bad things and had forgotten the good ones.

The study also concluded that the reason people think they are lucky is an upbeat outlook that helps them work a little harder and a little smarter to get what they want in life. People who remember mostly the bad things they experience and think they are unlucky are more likely to give up.

Everyone experiences good and bad things in life, but some people choose to remember more of the good things than the bad while others think mostly of the bad things rather than the good. What this means is that most people are a lot luckier than they think—if they would just choose to remember the lucky things that have happened to them and forget their misfortunes. Once you perceive yourself as lucky, it will be easier for others to see you that way. And if you are believed to be a lucky person, your chances of receiving "lucky" opportunities will increase.

Take this luck quiz alone or with someone else. Use a pad or talk into a tape recorder. Don't think too long about your answers. Just be honest. Then review your answers . . .

Mapping Your Luck Perspective

1. Name at least one person who you think is luckier than you are.
2. List three things that make that person luckier. More money? A more satisfying career? Fewer setbacks than you?
3. What do you think this person does to improve his or her luck?
4. Do you view this person positively or negatively?
5. If positively, do you respect the person because he or she deserves his or her good luck? If negatively, is it because you don't think the person deserves what he or she has achieved?

Conclusion: With your feelings out in the open, you should be able to see that the person you think is lucky actually takes steps to influence his or her good fortune. Your answers should also reveal to you that the person you think of as lucky actually just has more of what you want.

Mapping Your Recent Good Luck History

1. What is the luckiest thing that happened to you in the past week? The past month? The past year?

2. What area of life did this luck pertain to? Money?
   Career? Health? Love? Wriggling out of a dangerous
   situation?
3. Exactly what role did you play in influencing the good
   luck you mentioned in question 1? Name everything
   you did, even if it was just deciding to attend a meeting
   at which you met someone who offered you an
   opportunity.
4. Who else played a role in making your good luck
   happen? What did they do?
5. What aspects of your recent good luck were completely
   out of your control? Which were in your control?

Conclusion: Now you ought to realize that you're a pretty lucky person—probably much more fortunate than you previously thought—and that you played an active role in attracting that good luck.

Mapping Your Recent Bad Luck History

1. What was the *unluckiest* thing that happened to you in
   the past week? Past month? Past year?
2. What area of life did this unlucky event pertain to?
   Love? Money? Career? Health? Wriggling out of a
   dangerous situation?
3. Why exactly did you call it bad luck? What role did
   you play in influencing your misfortune? List everything, even if it was just a bad decision, that led to the
   problem.
4. In hindsight, if you could go back in time, what would
   you do differently if you had the opportunity to change
   the outcome? How would you think and behave
   differently?

Conclusion: Now you know that you aren't the random recipient of repeated misfortune, but that sometimes you play a role in attracting bad luck.

Having completed these exercises, you should now feel ready to play a bigger role in influencing your luck. Once you have reviewed your luck history, you'll see that being lucky really is a matter of how many unexpectedly good things happen to you over a short period of time. You'll also discover what your role or someone else's role was in making that luck happen. Most of all, you will realize that you are a lot luckier than you thought—and that how you feel about your past will guide your future luck. Reminding yourself each day how fortunate you are will make you begin to view yourself as lucky.

■ CHAPTER TWO ■

Good-Luck Myths and Realities

Any success requires both talent and luck.
And "luck" has to be helped along and provided by someone.

AYN RAND

There's an old expression: "We believe what we've always believed." What this means is that we're prisoners of our preconceived notions about ourselves and others. Such thinking can limit your luck if you view luck either as nonsense or as a force that is too powerful to consider influencing. Change the way you think about your luck and you will be much luckier than you are now.

People who view luck as nothing more than hard work probably work harder than they have to in life. People who are afraid to take control of their luck for fear of jinxing it probably fail to realize that good luck can be created and bad luck can be avoided. To improve the odds that more good things will happen to you, you must begin to feel and act lucky. To feel lucky, however, you first must stop believing that your luck is out of your control.

Here are the big myths about good luck that cause us to
think we have little influence over it . . .

• **Myth 1: Good luck is just another word for hard work and determination.** *Reality:* Hard work has nothing to do with good luck. If you want to succeed at anything in life, whether it's falling in love, making money, or advancing your career, you have to be as smart as or smarter than your rivals. Success requires it. But being smart isn't the same as working hard.

Not everyone who works hard is either successful or happy. Why is that? Because most people do nothing more than work hard and wait for good things to follow. It's almost as if they believe that hard work automatically entitles them to success. The problem with sheer hard work is that you wind up laboring so intensively that you miss spotting opportunities and taking advantage of them. As strange as it seems, there are also many people who work hard just so they can avoid dealing with such opportunities. Opportunity usually requires change, and change is scary. If you call a business contact whose name was given to you, you are going to come face to face with change if the opportunity works out. Change is tough because it means replacing the status quo with uncertainty.

The key question to ask yourself if you work hard is why you're doing it. If the answer is to push yourself in areas you haven't yet explored, that's great, because that type of hard work usually leads to exposure, new opportunities, and more good luck. But if you are working hard on the same projects you did several years ago, you're probably working hard to keep from growing and trying new things, which requires change.

To improve the odds that more great opportunities will come your way, you have to take steps to stack the deck in your favor. The late Sonny Bono is a good example of someone who exposed himself to as much change and opportunity as possible. No one ever said he sang well or looked good doing it. Was he the best restaurant owner ever? The best mayor of Palm Springs? A superior congressman? Probably not. Yet nearly everyone he met was only too happy to give him a break. At Bono's memorial service following his fatal skiing accident in late 1997, House Speaker Newt Gingrich said Bono was "a hard-working man who covered up his abilities." His self-effacing humor was a way to make opposing lawmakers feel comfortable.

Making others feel comfortable was Bono's specialty. He didn't take himself too seriously and his casual bluntness made him especially popular. *New York Post* columnist Steve Dunleavy probably said it best when he wrote that Bono's life was mostly a series of accidents—happy ones. Meeting Cher, his popular TV variety show, being elected mayor of Palm Springs and then to Congress—all "accidents," as Bono himself said. In reality, Bono was just darn good at looking lucky and taking advantage of the many opportunities that typically are made available to people who seem lucky.

• **Myth 2: You can't influence good luck . . . you just have to let life take its course.** *Reality:* If you let life take its course, you will certainly experience plenty of good and bad things. The problem is you may not experience the good things as quickly or as often as you'd like.

You can take some of the randomness out of your luck and change your good-luck/bad-luck ratio by taking a more active role in getting more positive things to happen to you. Poker champion Barbara Enright says that this is possible even in cards. Though you and your opponents are being dealt cards randomly, there is a great deal of critical thinking that determines your own play in poker. It's often the shrewdest player who wins. Luck certainly plays a role, but once the cards are dealt, the game is all psychology and who can remember who has what.

When Enright plays professionally, she works hard to control herself. She keeps herself from becoming angry or reckless by viewing setbacks as temporary. "When you feel like a loser, you act and play like a loser," says the two-time Ladies World Poker Champion. "It's all about character and what you think of yourself. I don't become annoyed too easily. There are a lot of jerks that misbehave at the table, but I try to block out that behavior, because I do not want anger to affect my play. Sometimes I even put on my headset and listen to music while I am playing."

Like poker, life demands total concentration. Even when things aren't going right, Enright waits for an opening by watching to see how opponents bet and by analyzing their body language. "Whenever you are among people who are as good as you are or better, your edge is your mind. If you can spot their flaws and identify your opportunities, you will come out ahead."

Lucky people also convince themselves that they deserve what they want—and that they are going to get it eventually. Then they focus on ways to make it happen, sooner rather than later. Most people waste time obsessing over whether or not it's really possible to achieve what they want most.

My brother, Danny, is good at making the impossible happen. He's a professional musician, so he must constantly scramble for work. His ideal gig is a one- or two-year contract playing piano at an established private club. The stability allows him to play other places while collecting a steady paycheck. It also keeps my mother happy. Several years ago, Danny told me he wanted the contract at one of the best-known and most exclusive clubs in New York City. Most pianists would have talked themselves out of trying, wondering whether they really were good enough to play there. Danny just walked in one morning, spoke to the manager, auditioned on the spot, and one week later he had his contract.

When the club elected new officers a year later, the officers chose a new pianist, and Danny was forced out. He could have internalized the rejection and moved on. But instead, Danny recognized the politics, lobbied the officers with whom he was friendly, and made friends with the new ones. The following year, he won back the contract—at better terms. Danny doesn't listen to other people's doubts, and he's better off for it. Shooting for the impossible requires him to shut out the nay-sayers. His nerve alone makes him seem lucky, and it forces the people who can help him to take notice.

• **Myth 3: To improve your luck, you need to meet the right people.** *Reality:* Meeting the right people is only half of it. If you can't create the right impression with the right people and get them to give you what you want—either immediately or eventually—meeting them is a waste of time. Meeting them can even be a detriment to your goal if those personal encounters are mishandled.

I witnessed a botched encounter at a child's birthday party. Once the kids were settled and baking cookies in the host's kitchen, several parents gathered in the living room to talk. No one really knew the others very well, since all of us were working parents who didn't have much time to socialize. A mother of one of the children cheerfully asked what everyone did for a living. After each parent responded, she was asked what she did. The woman said she had just lost her job as an advertising copywriter and that she was looking for work. She said she specialized in writing ads for high-end, luxury goods. She said she originally had chosen to work at a small ad agency because she thought she would have more autonomy. Obviously, she laughed, she was wrong, since she was now without a job.

Among the parents in the living room that afternoon, two said they were marketing executives. One was a senior advertising executive at a *Fortune* 500 media company and the other worked for a much smaller, direct-mail advertising firm. Over the next fifteen minutes, the woman focused her attention on the person at the smaller company, who had already said he wasn't in a position to help her. She all but ignored the executive from the large company.

When the woman left, I leaned over to the senior executive and whispered, "You're probably always in need of a part-time copywriter, aren't you?" "Yes," she whispered back, "but if the woman wasn't clever enough to ask me about myself and the opportunities at my company, she probably wasn't clever enough to do the job that I need done." Still baffled by the copywriter's failure to see the golden opportunity that I had recognized immediately, I asked the host of the birthday party about the jobless woman.

"Oh, she had a terrible experience at a large ad agency years ago, but it was actually a better job than the one at the smaller company she went to." Clearly the woman had faced some type of trauma at the large ad agency that caused her to forever rule out working for a large company again—even though the small ad agency was the one that had terminated her, and no two large companies are alike. But her fear of a large company had so blinded her that she didn't even bother to explore the opportunity sitting three feet away from her at the party. The woman's fear of failure and her subsequent mishandling of a key encounter dramatically limited her ability to make luck happen.

• **Myth 4: Good luck happens when you aggressively promote yourself.** *Reality:* Aggressively promoting yourself can brand you as obnoxious, and it can lead to bad luck. The more people you turn off, the fewer opportunities will be given to you and the less people will want to help you.

Promoting yourself is essential to attracting good luck, but there's a fine line between self-promotion and bragging. Skillful self-promotion excites and intrigues the listener. Bragging and pushiness have the opposite effect. They can be successful in getting you what you want—but you're also going to make enemies who can ruin your flow of luck. Where does self-promotion end and pushiness begin? Skillful self-promotion tells other people just enough about you and your accomplishments so that they come to their own conclusions. If you've left nothing to their imaginations, you were bragging.

Great public relations people and promoters know how to whet the appetite of editors and TV-news producers. They soft-sell, dangling just enough information so that the editors or producers whom they are trying to impress decide on their own to give their clients publicity. They seductively bait the hook—with smart, news-worthy information—in the hope that the "fish" will bite and give them what they want.

The same is true for the kind of self-promotion necessary to improve your luck. If you want to leave key people with the impression that you are lucky, not obnoxious, you have to create a positive impression without becoming offensive. You also must know when to use different approaches with different people.

Michael Levine is a prominent entertainment publicist who runs his own public relations firm in Los Angeles. He has been extremely successful by never promoting himself or his clients obnoxiously. Instead, he favors soft persistence. When he doesn't get a call returned by someone he's trying to reach, he will leave one gentle message a day on the contact's voice mail or answering machine. I have been on the receiving end of his patient persistence. His voice on the messages he leaves never sounds aggressive or angry, even when I haven't been able to call him back for a few days. He just sounds as if he's patiently waiting to talk to me. You can't help but call him back.

"By being gently persistent, you force people to pay attention to you without irritating them," Levine says. "In almost every case, the people you're trying to attract will pay attention. If I were to lose my cool or get pushy, I would blow what I am trying to accomplish long-term, which is a business relationship.

"The idea is to promote your message elegantly, so that the other person feels as if it is a gift that is wrapped in a Tiffany box. When a present arrives in a distinctive blue Tiffany box, we have a higher per-ceived value of the gift than if it came in no box or in a box of less prestige. The reason we react this way is not because we're psychological fools but because the box in and of itself says there is something special inside. A Tiffany box isn't garish or overdone. It simply says that the gift inside is of substance and high quality. Skillful promotion is very similar to that Tiffany box. You need to make the other person sense immediately that you're special—either in the relaxed way in which you handle yourself or the low-key but sharp way you look. If you can create that sensation, your qualities and achievements need little hard selling. They will speak for themselves, much like that box."

• **Myth 5: Good luck is just good timing**. *Reality:* Luck certainly requires good timing, but whether you wind up in the right place at the right time is most definitely within your control. Timing is not about coincidence. To be luckier than you are now, you have to take steps to be at the crossroads of opportunity when good fortune comes roaring through. It's even better if you're the only one at that intersection.

Angie Diehl-Jacobs has been an entertainment marketer for twenty years. She is now vice president of marketing at Universal Concerts, which is owned by one of the world's largest entertainment conglom-erates. She has seen her share of lucky people, from famous rock acts to skillful hangers-on. Yet the luckiest person she knows is the head of a major movie studio.

"He was always brilliant at being in the same place as opportunity. I remember early in his career he had the good fortune to be mentored by another movie-studio chief—an opportunity most people in the business miss out on. People assumed he was just lucky to be mentored by so powerful a person. But I know that he made that opportunity happen. He was prepared and understood that in the entertainment business most young Turks lack patience. In their rush to beat out rivals, they are more interested in hustling and showing each other how clever they are than learning from the old masters of the business. While hustling has its merits, it can also offend the older, more powerful people who have more respect for consideration and prudence.

"Of course, you always have to wrestle with which is more important—going for the throat or getting people to like you. It's a classic choice—do you want to be loved or respected? For this guy, it was more important to be loved first and then respected. His philosophy matched that of the older studio boss, who took him under his wing and taught him everything he knew.

"Had this guy only been interested in scoring as many fast points as possible, he would have missed the chance to be mentored by a legend. In my business, timing is about observing what's going on around you, sensing an opportunity, and stepping out into the opportunity's path so that it slams right into you. This guy was clever enough to allow himself to be schooled and mentored in a way that gave the older person satisfaction. He showed respect, he listened, he smiled at the right moments out of genuine passion, not out of sneakiness. He understood instinctively what every boss feels.

"I didn't get this until later in my career, when a boss remarked to me, 'I like people who like me.' It's so basic, yet it's something we forget in business, I suppose, because our egos are on the line. We always think, 'Well, if I'm talented and tenacious, I will make my own way.' Not necessarily. My boss did not promote people whom she perceived were not her supporters."

■CHAPTER THREE■

Why Some People Are Luckier Than Others

Luck is the sense to recognize an opportunity,
and the ability to take advantage of it.
Samuel Goldwyn

Lucky people are those for whom small miracles happen on a regular basis. We call them lucky because they don't seem to do much to attract their big breaks and they seem as dumbfounded as we are by their good fortune. They appear to do whatever makes them feel good—without much fear of the consequences. We are in awe of the limitlessness of their lives.

We all know people who skip through life being showered with opportunities and are never slowed by the bad things that happen to them. We love these people—but we hate them, too. However, instead of being jealous of lucky people, it's far more profitable to study their every move.

One of the luckiest people I know is my friend Ricky. We met for the first time in Boston in the mid-1970s as I was moving into my college dorm in my freshman year. Ricky and I lived next door to each other for nine months, and his ability to attract opportunity and dodge trouble was nothing short of amazing. Watching him carefully and studying his techniques taught me a great deal about luck and getting people to gladly give me what I want—and more. Ricky wasn't the smartest student in the world, but he was clever as a fox. While the rest of us were trying to be cool, worldly, or tough, Ricky was curious and naïve. By throwing himself on the mercy of others, he managed to get everyone to bend the rules for him. It was breathtaking. He never went without a date or party invitations. Rock concert tickets, backstage passes, used cars in mint condition, and even celebrity friends all gravitated toward him. He never bragged about these things and he always offered to share them with the rest of us.

Opportunity never stopped knocking for Ricky and trouble bounced off him all the time. That freshman year, Ricky broke nearly every one of the dorm's rules. He played his eight-track tapes too loud, virtually ran an open bar in his room, returned to the dorm after curfew, and pretty much did what he pleased. Since other guys in the dorm got into bigger trouble for much smaller infractions, I began to look hard at Ricky to see what it was about him that made him impervious to trouble and catnip for opportunity.

The closer I looked, the more I understood what was so special about Ricky. He was a good-looking guy, in a David Bowie sort of way, but his real magic was his ability to ride the surf of life, paddling every now and then to position himself in the current of other people's kindness. He didn't try to dominate conversations or be a know-it-all. If he had made anything look too difficult, the rest of us probably would not have thought him lucky. Instead, Ricky's strength was his ability to talk people into giving him what he wanted, and make them feel great while doing it. I can't remember Ricky ever being arrogant, angry, or negative. If he was denied what he wanted, he moved on. He even helped those who couldn't help him.

Ricky loved to play innocent, but he was a lot craftier than most of the people who knew him realized. One summer I remember Ricky telling us that what he wanted most in life was to be a play-by-play sports announcer for the Boston Red Sox. Everyone laughed and patted him on the back, telling him that he should go for it. That was the other thing about Ricky—you never wanted to discourage or disappoint him or tell him something wasn't possible. His career goal was so ridiculous that no one had the heart to burst his bubble. He was like a kid.

That summer, as the rest of us worked or swam by day and went out to discos at night, Ricky took a clunky tape recorder to Fenway Park and sat in the bleachers announcing every home game into his microphone. He would practice for hours, trying to overcome his slight lisp. Then he'd come back to the dorm and listen to his voice through the night, working hard to change the way he sounded. At parties, he would laugh along with everyone else who poked fun at what he was doing. Interestingly, he never discussed the details of his enterprise, nor did he openly express his anxieties or self-doubt, which I'm sure he felt.

One Sunday morning in late August, my roommate rushed in with a copy of the *Boston Globe*. There in the sports section was a photo of Ricky, smiling, with his tape recorder. A reporter had spotted him doing his weird announcing thing in the stands and thought Ricky would make a great story. A week after the article appeared, an executive at a Rhode Island radio station who saw the article called Ricky and, by the following spring, Ricky was doing play-by-play at Fenway Park on a part-time basis for the station. Just like that. Today, Ricky is a TV sportscaster and sportswriter in southern California.

Here's what I learned by watching Ricky.
These "luck-making" lessons can work for anyone . . .

• **Think smart and play dumb.** If you know what you want, don't pretend you know how to get there. People like to help and support those who seem innocent and vulnerable.

• **Don't waste time perfecting what you do.** You don't have to be the world's best to get a break. You just have to be good enough. Equally important is whether you can convince others that you are worthy of their help and will make great use of your breaks. Ricky never got rid of his lisp completely nor smoothed out his announcing. But he got good enough, and it was his sheer optimism and eagerness that landed him a shot writing for magazines and reporting on television. Focus on creating the next opportunity. Perfection will come in time.

• **Believe with all your heart that people are going to give you what you want, eventually.** If you set your mind to making good luck happen, it will. If you believe that it will happen, people will give it to you because they will see how much you want it. Years later, Ricky told me the secret of his determination against long odds. "I tell myself, 'I'm going to get what I want. The people who have what I need just don't know yet that they're going to give it to me. But they will.'"

• **Forget about grudges—they're not worth it.** Ricky faced plenty of letdowns and setbacks in college but he never held them against anyone. Grudges are a waste of energy, Ricky said. You spend too much time trying to strike back—time that could have been used to make something else happen for you. Besides, you pleasantly surprise people when you let them off the hook. They'll want to help you the next time, just to stop feeling guilty.

• **Do favors without making other people feel as if they owe you anything.** Ricky would give other people the shirt off his back. He wasn't a fool. Ricky knew his strategy would create the impression that he was so lucky, he didn't need the shirt or anything he owned. When someone behaves this way, you get the feeling the person could always replace what he or she gave up just by wishing for it. When Ricky said, "If you want it, take it. I'll get another one," he accomplished three things at once: First, you felt great that he gave you something you wanted. Second, you felt you owed him one. And third, you felt he was lucky. That was the strange part. Anyone who would give up a blazer, tickets to Fleetwood Mac, or even fix you up with a woman he had dated must have some magical power to get more where that came from.

It's human nature to keep the things we cherish, not to give them up. By giving them away, Ricky exhibited an enormous amount of self-confidence. The funny thing was that if the jacket looked great on you, you told people it was Ricky's. When you told people you went to see Fleetwood Mac, you mentioned that Ricky got you the tickets. When Ricky fixed you up with a friend, you usually spent part of the evening talking about what a great guy Ricky was.

What's true for Ricky, I learned, is true for most everyone else. Being lucky—experiencing good luck on a regular basis—is about consciously becoming more appealing without making people think you're a soft touch or an idiot. Behave like Ricky and you'll elicit more favors, encouragement, admiration, and breaks from a wider range of people. When this happens, you'll be thought of as lucky, and that's exactly where you want to be.

Why I'm a Lucky Guy

Talk to successful people about their achievements and they will tell you the accomplishments were the result of hard work or lots of luck or both. Probe a little further and ask them to be specific, and you will hear about the many things they did to make their lucky breaks happen.

In some cases, you'll discover that these people got their breaks by getting friends, strangers, colleagues, and even adversaries to give them what they wanted. This is a crucial point. While many people work harder than necessary to achieve success and others do nothing but wish for opportunity to come their way, lucky people get others to offer them chances to get what they want.

Many people say I'm lucky, and I suppose I am. Throughout my life, I have had the good fortune to be exposed to many lucky people. By observing and following their behavior, I have done well, and I'm happy. While I'm fully aware that the trappings of my life could disappear in a flash, I also know that the right outlook on life has everything to do with good fortune. I have always made sure to create opportunities and to pounce on the best ones that have come my way. And my timing has always been excellent.

I won my first job as a copyboy in the editorial page department of the *New York Times* when I was a sophomore in college. I was part of my university's work-study program, and I got the *Times* job because I brought my portfolio of published articles to my interview and the other candidates did not. I was also extremely enthusiastic about the job and the *Times,* and that enthusiasm played a big role in helping me land the job. I showed that I had wanted the job more than everyone else who had interviewed.

When John Oakes, my boss, left as editorial page editor just after I started, Max Frankel, who later would become the newspaper's top editor, took over. I was concerned that my work-study position would be dissolved. Refusing to leave my fate to chance, I wrote Max a heartfelt letter explaining why I loved working at the newspaper and why working for him would provide me with an invaluable experience. No one asked me to write the letter. It just seemed like the smart thing to do. Soon afterward I was told that my position would be preserved.

Appreciating the break, I went out of my way to become invaluable. When Max started as editorial page editor he needed a desk because John Oakes had taken his with him to his new office. While Max waited for his new desk to be delivered, he worked for the first week at his secretary's desk. When I overheard his secretary on the phone struggling to get a temporary desk delivered, I told her I would find one. I went to the freight elevator and asked the guys I knew if there was a decent-sized desk in the building that we could bring up. They said there was a new one being delivered to someone in the advertising department, and that they would bring up the desk that the person was giving up. Up came the desk, and I'll never forget Max's secretary's face when it arrived fifteen minutes after we spoke. "How did you do that?" Max asked me, laughing.

The lesson I learned was that successful people love people who hustle and solve problems creatively.

While I was still in college, I had my first bylined article in the *New York Times*. I had just reported a story on the former death house at Sing Sing Prison in Ossining, New York, where many people had been electrocuted. At the time, the structure was being used as office space to process furloughed prisoners. Nothing sells like irony, and this story was about a place that had been a last stop for prisoners but now was processing them back into society. I asked Max if he would edit my copy before I turned it in. He generously made time for me, and my article was published. The lesson here was never be afraid to ask for help from the most powerful people you know when you're trying to improve your luck. When I graduated from college, Max took the unprecedented step of offering me the job of deputy editor of the Letters to the Editor page for the summer. I was just twenty-four years old.

Even meeting my wife at the *New York Times* was a case of making good luck happen—in this instance, seizing an opportunity that seemed to come miraculously out of nowhere. Several weeks before I planned to leave the *Times* in 1985 to freelance, I needed an upcoming issue of the *Times Sunday Magazine* in which my name was to appear. I called a woman in the advertising department, who said that boxes of the magazine I was looking for were right outside her office. So I went to her office to get a few copies. We chatted for a few minutes, I asked her for her phone number, and eight months later we were married.

Weeks after leaving the *Times,* I won a lucrative magazine consulting assignment because the editorial page editor at *New York Newsday,* who had met me once, recommended me for the job. Perfect timing, but it didn't hurt that before I met him, I had sent him a long list of editorial ideas, some of which eventually were adopted by the newspaper. So he thought of me when the consulting job came up. A few weeks after the consulting job ended, I was hired as an editor at *Adweek,* after cold-calling the editor-in-chief. The magazine had lost an editor that day. Great timing, but I had improved my odds of success by reading the magazine cover to cover that morning and was able to discuss it in detail on the phone with the editor.

My appearance on ABC's *Nightline* several years later occurred because the editor-in-chief at one of *Adweek's* marketing publications was on vacation and I was his deputy. When asked on the phone by the show's producer if I could appear in the editor's place to talk about the merits of oat bran, I said yes. I was only twenty-nine, but I knew that the worst that could happen was I would make a mistake on TV.

I've also jumped at opportunities when it didn't seem to my friends as if the career move was a good one. Kate White, who has been editor-in-chief of *Child, McCall's, Redbook,* and now *Cosmopolitan,* hired me in 1990 as business editor when she was editor-in-chief of

Working Woman. Though the magazine had an all-female staff at the time, she hired me, she said, because my body language had asked for the job.

Two years later, I was interviewed on NBC's *Today* show because a controversial article I had developed and edited about what high-level executive men dislike most about women in the workplace was published during Anita Hill's testimony against Clarence Thomas. A complete coincidence, but when asked to appear on live TV, I didn't hesitate for a minute. I knew that the most frightening experiences often teach you the most about yourself and how far you can go.

Even meeting Martin Edelston, president of Boardroom Inc. and owner of the newsletters I edit now—*Bottom Line/Personal* and *Moneysworth*—was an instance of making good luck happen. An executive recruiter called me just when I was ready for a new challenge. But this was no chance call. I had spent years developing a close relationship with this recruiter, so that when opportunities came up, I would be among the first people who would come to mind.

In almost every case I can think of, I have been able to attract golden opportunities and turn them into positive career moves by thinking ahead. Working for brilliant, successful people allowed me to see firsthand how they operate, what they look for in others, and how they make decisions and allocate their time so that they can make more luck for themselves.

If you look at the people you know who seem to get what they want over and over again, you'll notice they all have a similar trait: They do a fantastic job of convincing other people that good things leap out of nowhere and cling to them. This is the biggest secret that all lucky people share. They all know that when they seem lucky, more people will want to help them. Lucky people aren't really any more spiritually blessed or chosen than anyone else. They just behave in specific ways that make us think they are.

Lucky Stiffs Work Smart and Plead Innocent

All lucky people have two things in common: First, they are constantly thinking up creative ways to improve the odds that more in life will go their way. Second, when they get what they want, they act as baffled as others are by their good fortune. It's precisely this artful combination of behind-the-scenes assertiveness coupled with onstage humility that makes them seem lucky. Micromanage the forces that can steer good luck your way—and then act like an innocent victim when good fortune leaps into your arms.

My agent, Sheree Bykofsky, won $34,000 on *Wheel of Fortune* several years ago. Was it luck? Sure, Sheree would be the first to tell you that having the giant wheel stop where it did was all luck. Having opponents who made mistakes was lucky, too. But I know what Sheree did behind the scenes to get on the show in the first place, and her strategies were extremely clever.

Sheree wrote to the show on a whim, asking to be a contestant. When she was sent a postcard telling her when and where to appear for an audition, she left little to fate. Instead of just showing up unprepared, she spent the weeks leading up to the audition watching tapes of the show and studying contestants' body language and reactions. She noticed that the women never dressed in all black or white but often wore solid blue or green and very little jewelry. Their dresses also had high necklines. She took notes on how they clapped and yelled and what they looked like when they spun the wheel and the rubber arrow pointed to "Bankrupt."

At the audition, she was one of about two hundred hopefuls from whom just five would be chosen. After making the cut at several levels of interviews, the producers asked her to play a few mock games. She clapped and screamed, and used the right game-show body language that she had so meticulously observed. Her strategy worked. In the end, she became one of the bubbly contestants chosen. Sheree made luck happen by behaving like a successful contestant. She influenced the odds of getting in the game by convincing the producers to give her what she wanted.

Other people improve the odds of being lucky by refusing to give in to either negativity or bragging. Ken Flaton, one of the country's top professional poker players and winner of the $500,000 first prize at the U.S. Poker Championship in Atlantic City several years ago, says that coming out ahead when you can't control everything happening around you depends on how well you take advantage of the opportunities that come your way.

"To win, I have to stay focused. I keep my head clear by living by two important rules: I push negativity out of my head and I always avoid negative people. I don't think you can be a great poker player and be a negative person. When I'm playing, I'm constantly thinking of my wife and son, and how much I love them. That blocks out any anger or anxiety.

"I want other players to think I'm lucky, so I never brag. If I did, my opponents would be jealous and play harder and probably smarter just to beat me. Negativity and bragging lead to failure. Once you start putting yourself or others down, it's hard to stop. Soon you're expecting everything to go against you and you're blaming others for your problems. Bragging leads to overstating your true abilities. Eventually you start to believe your own lies and take risks you shouldn't have."

Flaton's insights help to explain how important a good attitude and a sense of perspective are. "When you're lucky," Flaton says, "people give you what you want, or they get so jealous that they make mistakes. If you can keep cool, you'll always come out ahead."

The Bandwagon Effect—
Why Luck Loves Lucky People

Good things keep happening to people we think of as lucky—even though they suffer the same temporary setbacks we do. Why? Because luck loves lucky people. This phenomenon is a key concept for anyone trying to improve his or her luck. The luckier you seem, the more people will want to help and protect you.

Anyone who wants to be lucky must reach a point where good things happen to them all the time. Once you're considered someone who attracts good things, the more good things will find their way to you. It's what Andy Pargh calls the "Bandwagon Effect." Andy is one of the nicest and most easy-going people I know. He reviews gadgets and electronics and then writes a nationally syndicated column telling consumers which ones he likes best. He also appears regularly on the *Today* show, writes a column in *USA Today,* and edits a new magazine on his favorite new products. He's forty-four years old, and his rise from local television guest in Tennessee to the expert known nationally as "The Gadget Guru" has been rapid. The secret of his success, he told me, has been to work hard to make everything look easy and make everyone else look good.

"Hey, I'm not the smartest guy in the world," Andy says. "There are plenty of people out there who review new electronics. The difference is that my staff and I work hard to make what I do seem effortless. This not only makes me seem lucky to the people I do business with but also makes their lives easier. As a result, I'm always high on their lists when opportunities come up. It's amazing how many people will line up and want to work with you once they know their competitors are already on your good side. Everyone wants what the other guy has. Once enough people climb aboard your bandwagon, others will also want to climb on. Then it's just a matter of fielding and managing your opportunities."

Andy says he makes it a point never to be the one who loses his cool or lands on other people's revenge lists. "It's a big, big mistake trying to make yourself popular by screwing over other people or your competitors. You poison your luck by doing that. It's much more profitable to simply succeed and let the powers that be know you've succeeded. Once they see that you're happy and that you regularly get what you want, they'll want to be associated with you. My staff and I work like dogs, yet people think I coast through life. I think it has to do with the fact that I seem so relaxed. You have to work hard at making it seem as if nothing bothers you."

Andy's right. If you can do a commendable job and create the impression that your talent is a gift, more lucky things will happen to you—even when you face inevitable setbacks. For as long as I've known Andy, he has always been incredibly upbeat, helpful, professional, and relaxed. As we know, creating that kind of impression takes effort. You have to be up when you are down, you can't dwell on life's disappointments, and you have to make people feel great about knowing you. Andy has the ability to make people want to give him whatever he wants because he always makes the first move to help them. Whenever Andy calls, just the sound of his voice implies, "Tell me how I can help you—nothing would give me more pleasure."

When you make life easy for others, you become a guardian angel—someone who can be counted on for great work and little hassle. Once you have that reputation, people will give you whatever you want to keep you in their corner.

■CHAPTER FOUR■

Luck-Making Habits That Pay Off

Somewhere along the line I made the switch and was able to look at
the bright side rather than the dark side all the time.
Now I look at everything I have and think how lucky I am.

ACTRESS MICHELLE PFEIFFER

The amount of good luck you receive in life is directly related to how lucky you think you are. The more you believe that good things routinely come your way, the luckier you will behave, and the more people will want to help you.

Think lucky, and your optimism will automatically show on your face and in how you carry yourself. Believe you are lucky, and you will feel invincible—convinced that a force is protecting you from the misfortunes others suffer. Your optimism and self-pride will soar and be evident to everyone you meet. A lucky attitude seductively draws people near and enlists them in your cause.

To think and behave lucky, you must develop a special set of habits that will become the basis for everything you say and do. Practice these habits, and you will acquire lucky instincts and reflexes.

Every lucky person I know lives by these essential habits that lay the foundation for attracting good luck.

Don't Play the Blame Game, and Always Bury Your Grudges

I'm always amazed by people who resist taking responsibility for their problems or setbacks. Instead, they instantly blame others because it feels good to let themselves off the hook. Sure, holding yourself accountable feels terrible because you come face to face with your flaws. But once you start blaming others, it becomes a habit that is difficult to kick.

Although some things are indeed the fault of others, playing the blame game is always corrosive to your luck. Eventually you begin rationalizing mistakes out loud to others. For example, you can't get your work done so you blame the number of meetings you must attend or the interruptions by people on your staff. Or you neglect to spend enough time telling people exactly how you want a finished project to look and then blame them when the completed assignment doesn't meet your standards.

When you openly blame others rather than holding yourself accountable, you leave a negative impression. In effect you're saying, "It's never me; I'm never to blame," and no one wants to help people who make excuses. Excuses always sound like whining. And even when excuses are explanations, they are always interpreted as cop-outs. Making excuses is the language of weasels, liars, and losers—not winners. When you hear professional athletes being interviewed after a game on TV, you never hear them blame the other side for the loss. They may compliment the other team for being aggressive and tough, but you'll never hear a professional athlete say, "If I only had the ball more often," or, "The sun was way too bright out there." Never. The reason they don't do that is that they have been trained to reject excuses because excuses are self-defeating. Once you start making them, you neglect to take steps to improve your own performance or behavior.

What to tell yourself every day to keep from blaming others . . .

- **Mistakes are natural. Learn from them.**
- **When things don't work out, write down what you'll do differently the next time.**
- **Say those things out loud or into a tape recorder.**
- **Practice saying out loud, "It was my fault. Let me see how I can fix it."**

- **Tell yourself that the more you take responsibility for problems that were within your control, the luckier you will become.** Accepting responsibility for things that were under your control is always viewed as noble behavior. You are immediately someone of character and worthy of help, and people will admire your strength and courage. Accepting blame also tells people you are honest, which makes them want to offer you opportunities. If accepting blame makes you seem a little flawed, that's fine. You need to seem a little imperfect in order to receive assistance. When in doubt about taking responsibility for a mistake, take it. You'll always be admired for it.

What if the mistake was unmistakably someone else's? Should you hold a grudge? Some people believe that holding a grudge is a positive force, because it motivates us to be more aggressive and competitive. Maybe so, but holding a grudge won't make you lucky, only unlucky. When you hold a grudge against someone who you believe hurt you or tried to hurt you, you limit your opportunities.

Carrying around grudges leads to stress, anger, and eventually behavior that will ruin your image in the eyes of those who can help you most. Hostile behavior isn't easily forgotten by the people who witness it or hear about it. In the long term, overly emotional behavior is never viewed as a positive. You may get fast results, but you will have made many people afraid of you. Others will be unwilling to share with you great opportunities.

A grudge starts out as a highly charged private emotion, but eventually it finds its way out into the open, either through gossip or by your actions. As soon as your grudge becomes evident, you will have poisoned your well. People may continue to help you, but their assistance is usually motivated by their desire to see you become angrier and more malicious toward the person for whom you hold a vendetta.

Forcing yourself to drop grudges will free you to think positively and concentrate on what's important, which in turn promotes an open, honest, and positive image.

Secrets of kicking the grudge habit . . .

• **Sidestep or ignore people who hurt you.** Tell yourself that whatever they have done to hinder you was just an indirect way of helping you. Imagine they have made you stronger and more resourceful.

• **Never talk openly about people you dislike.** Your grudge will just grow, and your image will suffer.

• **If you must talk about the offending person, cast him or her in a positive light:** "I wish that person were nicer. She's probably under a great deal of pressure."

When you bury your grudges—or at least control them—you will become more upbeat, and people will want to be around you and help you become successful.

Mean What You Say,
and Avoid Saying Anything Mean

Sincere compliments always make people feel good, which will cause them to feel good about you. Some people think the art of delivering a compliment is nothing more than flattery—a sleazy attempt to manipulate or brown-nose someone into giving you something. But there's a big difference between complimenting and flattering. A compliment is backed by sincerity, and there is nothing wrong with making people feel good when you mean what you're saying.

Lucky people are masters at expressing themselves when delivering a compliment. Their praise always feels natural because they truly believe in their words. When someone we think of as lucky says something complimentary to us, we never stop to ask about his or her motive. We feel great, no questions asked, because we know they are sincere. We also want to give them whatever they want.

So, the first step in delivering any compliment is to truly mean what you say. Otherwise you're better off not saying anything. The second step is to compliment only when it will be well-received. For example, you may be completely honest when you praise someone's figure, but you're going to leave a negative impression of yourself if the person is overweight and knows it. The most powerful compliments are those that praise what *isn't* obvious. Then your praise is personal, sincere, and also warmly received. Once your compliment is warmly received, *you* will be warmly received and more likely to be helped by others.

Here are a handful of potent compliments,
but don't say them unless your heart is in them . . .

- **Saying something nice about a person's clothes. Clothes are extensions of our personalities and no one is ever completely secure about either of them.**

- Saying something nice about a person's hairstyle. Same reasons.
- Praising someone's work and level of energy.
- Praising someone's taste in personal items, such as their choice of furnishings, artwork, music, or food.
- Praising someone's generosity.
- Praising those things that a person works hard to perfect, such as work habits, reports, or presentations.

Compliments that usually backfire . . .

- **Complimenting someone's loss of weight.** Too personal. It also means you thought they were fat in the past.
- **Complimenting someone on how they handled a situation gone bad.** No one wants pity or to be reminded of a tough situation they're probably trying to forget.
- **Complimenting someone on something they did that was mean, like firing someone or criticizing a coworker at a meeting.** Those types of things disgust most people, and they don't want to be reminded of them.
- **Complimenting someone's eyes.** Sounds great in the movies, but it always sounds fake in real life.
- **Complimenting someone's sense of humor.** Saying "You're so funny" puts people on the defensive. Say "That's funny," but never "You are funny."
- **Complimenting someone on the things they have that they may be afraid of losing, like cute girlfriends or boyfriends.**

Lucky people really know how to deliver a compliment. They know how and when to insist that their praise is true. They know that sometimes delivering a sincere compliment isn't enough. You have to drive it home to emphasize your sincerity. For example, saying, "I'm serious, you're amazing when it comes to getting things done—really," overcomes the person's humility and goes straight to the heart. The trick is knowing when to stop before a truly sincere comment sounds fake.

When your compliment is sincere and truly touches another person, that person feels great about you. The more people you can make feel great about you, the better your chances of attracting more opportunities. People like helping those who make them feel good about themselves. They tend to think of such people as special—even lucky.

Don't Be a Know-It-All

This is one of the hardest habits to develop. If you're reading this book, you're obviously smart, and smart people like to show off their knowledge. But showing off your smarts is addictive. You can become so caught up in your own brilliance that you stop listening to others. You drown out other voices and think your way is the only way.

Know-it-alls aren't very likable or lucky for two reasons: Their behavior and attitude isolate them from people who can help them. And they seem too self-sufficient, which removes them as candidates for help. In other words, you can be too smart for your own good.

Secrets of reformed know-it-alls . . .

• **Ask questions instead of making statements.** Every time you feel the urge to pontificate, lecture, or follow someone else's story with one of your own, ask a question. One lucky person I know calls this the "Why Factor." Whenever he has the urge to cut the other person off with a comment of his own, he says, instead, "That's interesting . . . why?"

• **Train yourself to listen to the answers.** In my line of work as an editor and writer, I have come to know a great many reporters. The best reporters I know are great listeners. They've trained themselves to listen for great quotes, new angles, and insights into the material they are working on. One way to force yourself to listen is to take notes. One lucky person I know puts his fingers to his lips as he listens, a move that acts as a reminder to remain silent. Another lucky individual who used to be guilty of being a know-it-all says he concentrates on what the other person is saying by imagining he is in his car. When someone is talking, he mentally shifts into neutral and coasts, which helps him put his mind in a receptive state.

• **Stop trying to have the last word.** Know-it-alls are notorious for topping stories with their own anecdotes: "It's funny you should say that, because your story reminds me of the time . . ." Such anecdotes are rarely appreciated, even if they are great ones. You always come off as if you're trying to top the other person's story, and very often you eclipse the joy the other person had by telling it. Recognize that people who must always have the last word or seem right aren't much fun to be around or help. If you become genuinely interested in what other people have to say, you will be privy to information that could lead to golden opportunities.

• **Learn to laugh at yourself.** If you take yourself too seriously, no one will think you're lucky. Realize that everyone has quirks or habits that amuse other people. Once you accept this fact, you'll be able to laugh along and not become too offended by the gentle barbs hurled at you. Lucky friends of mine say that when people poke fun at them, they make sure they are the first ones to laugh, as painful as that might be. They may even add a self-deprecating zinger to drive home the point and show that there are no hard feelings. When people poke gentle fun at you, it's often because they either envy you or are so comfortable around you that they have no trouble razzing you. Treat these quips as compliments, not as malicious attacks or betrayals. If you do find yourself viewing them as attacks, you may be taking yourself too seriously.

Appreciate What You Have While
Seeking What You Don't Have

In our quest to make life go our way, we often lose sight of the many great things that have already happened to us. It's human nature to be upset about not getting what we want rather than appreciating what we have already. A woman I know who worked in the office of a tough boss had the sunniest attitude. She was always smiling and willing to help out. She never snapped, never seemed to be in a bad mood.

When I asked her one day how she could be in such a great mood all the time, she said, "Oh, everything here is easy. My son has just gone through chemotherapy. When you have that going on in your life, everything else falls into perspective. You quickly realize that the stuff that seems stressful or hard really isn't that tough. Most of it goes away the next day or week."

As you set out to improve your luck, think hard about what you have achieved so far, and be grateful for it. That's not to say that you should be happy to sit back and forget about trying to make your dreams come true. But if you recognize that you already have many great things and that life could get much worse for you overnight, your attitude about life and your goals will change. When you appreciate what you have and are grateful for your health, your home, the love of your family, and your talents and skills, you won't agonize over your bad breaks or give up when things don't go your way. Instead, you'll see the vivid pattern of your good fortune and focus on making more of it come your way.

One way to put your life into perspective is to read the foreign pages of the *New York Times* or any other national newspaper. I defy anyone to read about the slaughter and destruction of innocent people in Africa or Eastern Europe and then agonize over having to wait in line at the store or become miserable over a mistake made at work.

When you compare your "hardships" with those of people whose lives are much more difficult, your life won't seem so miserable.

Here are some other exercises for appreciating what you have . . .

• **It's a wonderful life**. Imagine that tomorrow, when you awaken in the morning, everything you have now is gone. Your health, your talents, skills, job, your family—everything. Wouldn't your first thought be to wish it all back? Then remember that you have all of those things right now.

• **Imagine that you are ninety-five years old.** Looking back, what would you appreciate about your age now? What would you wish you had taken advantage of?

• **Think about your less fortunate friends.** What are you grateful for that others may not have as much of—loving relationships, special attributes, a creative spirit?

• **Take a closer look at your kids.** Think about the joy they bring you—not the stress or consternation. When you're old and gray, you're going to wish they called more, and you'll give anything to have them back at that young age.

Lucky people are always thinking about their current lives in relation to the less fortunate lives of others. It makes them realize how good they have it, and they are quick to recognize just how lucky they are. When you recognize how good you have it, you will automatically feel much more upbeat about what you're doing and where you're going. The more upbeat you look and sound, the more people will want to help you get what you want. It's that simple.

Look the Part

Looking lucky isn't about getting dressed up or wearing expensive clothes or looking trendy. Looking lucky is about *neatness*.

How crisp you look is much more important than you think. Dress-down days at work have created a new tolerance for informality and have presented a wonderful opportunity for people to stand out. When people dress down, the tendency is to dress further and further down until Friday looks like Sunday afternoon. Slacks turn into chinos, which turn into neat jeans, and eventually any old jeans. Crisp shirts turn into pullovers and even sweatshirts. Being noticed for neatness has never been easier.

The importance of looking neat and well-groomed isn't about ego and self-esteem. The reason it pays to look good is that you make other people feel good. When you've taken the time to look good, you're showing respect for those around you. You're enhancing their environment with color and order, and leaving them feeling good about you and themselves.

Looking lucky is a matter of personal style, but no one who dresses as if they were home ever looks lucky—unless they own the company or are worth a billion dollars. If you're looking for others to provide you with career opportunities or set you up on dates, you must look distinctive and sharp enough so that they are proud to put you in play.

I know a prominent woman who throws elaborate parties for the political and cultural elite. The whole point of those parties, she told me recently, isn't to show off her house, which is a magnificent brownstone. Instead, she likes everything to be perfect so that her guests feel special and have a great time. If people are talking about her house when they leave, my friend says, she has done something wrong. She wants her guests to leave saying, "Gee, what a great time. What great food. What great people. It's always so much fun seeing them."

Looking lucky is about much the same thing. The purpose of dressing neatly and colorfully isn't to show people how stylish you are or how much money you have. It's about making people feel great when they see you. Color and coordination have a pleasing effect on people, psychologically. When you're well-groomed and you dress attractively, others feel warm toward you because their senses are stimulated in a positive way.

To find out how far you have to go to dress for opportunity,
I took a poll among my lucky friends. I asked them for
the most important clothing and grooming do's and don'ts
that would influence them to help or deny someone an
opportunity. Here's what they told me . . .

- DO make sure your hair is well-groomed. How you take care of your hair says a lot about your work habits and ambition.
- DO make sure your shoes are shined. Nothing says "I'm lucky" louder than a great-looking pair of shoes.
- DO make sure that shirts are laundered and pressed, blouses are dry-cleaned, and that you wear tasteful accessories. If your shirt, blouse, shoes, and belt are sharp, the suit you're wearing won't even matter.
- DO make sure your eyeglass frames make a statement about your intelligence, not your fashion sense.
- DON'T dress down, even on Fridays or bad-weather days. A dressy look will make people feel great when the weather is lousy.
- DON'T try to dress younger than your age.
- DON'T wear loud ties (men) or huge earrings (women).
- Avoid a trendy or retro look. Too much style distracts from the power of your personality and intelligence.

Be Patient

Lucky people never rest. They take breaks, but they're always on the move, hunting for opportunities or contacts. Lucky people are always trying to advance themselves, and they take deadlines seriously. They also know when it pays to coast for a while.

A friend of mine once became bitter when his company hired someone with less experience for a job at the same level. The boss said he thought the department needed some youth. As soon as the person was hired, the boss started singing his praises, which angered many of the other people. My friend knew that the boss was wrong. He had noticed immediately that the person had several major character flaws. For one, he wasn't very smart politically. Second, he wasn't very efficient when it came to doing the job. Third, he was pompous, which my friend knew eventually would put him in conflict with the boss.

My friend said at the time that he had two choices. He could go head to head with the person, challenging him at every meeting and setting up a major rivalry, or he could help the person and not make a fuss. He said he wasn't comfortable with either choice, so I recommended a middle ground. I suggested he let the person "run out the line." I don't fish, but sometimes the way to win is to let the fish run until it gets tired. Then you start reeling it in. My advice was two-fold: "If this person is great at his job, you will benefit because you're smart and you'll bond with him. If he stinks, he'll make mistakes, and those mistakes eventually will cost him."

So my friend supported the person and let people know he was helping out. When the person eventually was fired, my friend was promoted. People at the company thought my friend was lucky to survive. His secret, he told me, was to provide just enough support to seem congenial and to keep a low profile while waiting out the clock. Had he become openly bitter, or sabotaged the person, the person may still have been fired but my friend would have been viewed as the cause. It would have been clear that his motives were selfish rather than for the larger good of the company.

Here are some of the secrets of lucky people I know who beat rivals by putting time on their side . . .

- **Identify your rivals' flaws.**
- **Watch to see whether others recognize those flaws.**
- **Do what you're asked to support your rival.**
- **Never bad-mouth your rival.**
- **If your rival succeeds, be an ally. If he or she fails, your value will soar because you'll be viewed as the team player you are. Either way, you wind up getting what you want—and looking lucky.**

Fight Off Feelings of Envy at All Costs

One of the most self-destructive emotions is envy. It makes us bitter, undercutting our positive energy and forcing us to make costly mistakes that compromise our luck and opportunities. Once you seem like a jealous person, you will no longer be thought of as lucky. Only unlucky people become bitter and petty about the good fortune of others.

Some people I know think that jealousy is a good thing, that it drives you to achieve your goals, and that if you aren't envious of other people you won't have the fire in your belly that's needed to succeed.

I disagree. Envy frequently pushes us into setting premature or completely unreachable goals. Envy also can put you in competition with the wrong people, setting you up for failure and self-hatred. In love, we often become jealous when someone else is with a man or woman who we think should be with us. At work, we can become envious of the person who has an intimate and natural relationship with our manager or boss. We want that too. People long for the cars, houses, opportunities that other people have because they think those things will make them happy. Such desires can be positive, provided you don't become obsessed and blinded by them. But too often, envy leads to bad-mouthing the people who have what we want, which causes us to look petty, angry, and not very lucky. Envy is an acidic emotion that quickly leads to an outlook that corrodes our luck.

What to tell yourself to suppress or eliminate
feelings of envy . . .

- **I'm only in competition with myself.**
- **Eventually I will have what I want.**
- **Who knows—maybe what the other person has that I want isn't as great as I think it is.**
- **What are the great things that I have already that other people wish they had?**

Relax—Tomorrow's Another Day

When life doesn't go your way, chalk it up to a rough day and move on. You have to. Otherwise you can go crazy. As bad as something is on one particular day, it almost always is brighter the next day. What you can't solve now often can be solved with a little perspective and sleep.

There are days when I must edit three or four articles a day. Many of these articles need to be reorganized, with a new opening paragraph. Sometimes the solution flies off my fingers. Other times I sit there staring at the screen, wondering whether I can even form a sentence. When that feeling sets in, I close up the file on my computer screen and move on. Interestingly, when I pick up the copy the next day, much of what I couldn't solve in an hour's time comes within minutes.

Everyone has experienced those days when shirt buttons pop off, stockings run, and your timing never seems to be right. Those missteps frequently come in clusters but soon right themselves as we gain our equilibrium.

If you automatically assume that small problems will go away by themselves, you'll avoid wasting time and energy trying to solve them immediately. All of the most successful, lucky people I know understand this concept. They rarely agonize over what they can't solve immediately. When a big managerial problem lands in their office—such as two people on their staff who aren't getting along—they rarely act on it immediately. They let emotions cool first. Or they say they will get right on it but let a little time pass so that the emotional heat, which could have been explosive if confronted immediately, has had time to burn off.

Giving problems time to work themselves out also keeps you from becoming stressed out. Martin Edelston, president of Boardroom Inc., is a master at this. Watching him run his ninety-employee company is truly amazing. He faces critical personnel and business decisions every day, yet he rarely makes a bad decision. His secret? The more sensitive the problem, the more time he takes to think through all of the problem's angles and the more he forces everyone involved to relax. Only when he's detached and at ease and has examined every angle can he exercise good judgment and make solid decisions.

Here's how successful people use a relaxed attitude to deal with tricky problems and put them in perspective . . .

• **Tell yourself that no problem is so important that it must be resolved immediately.** It only seems that way because people are telling you that's the case.

• **Ask questions, and consider every drawback and advantage.** Outline them in a memo to yourself, if necessary.

• **Learn to relax.** Tension is the major cause of stress. If you tell yourself to slow down when the going gets rough, breathe deeply, and postpone your decisions, you will find that many problems solve themselves without your having to compromise your lucky image.

When you have a mindset that laughs off difficulty and views all problems as solvable, you make other people relax and feel good about you. As they relax, their estimation of you rises. You appear stronger, wiser, and luckier.

■CHAPTER FIVE■

Becoming a Luck Magnet— Goals, Contacts, and Timing

Luck is believing you're lucky.

TENNESSEE WILLIAMS

Once you've started to change your mindset, the next step is to identify your dreams and the people who can help you realize them. Too many people try to make good luck happen without having much of a plan. They just wait until an opportunity crosses their path and then they try to jump on it. A more effective way to manage the flow of opportunities is to know what you want and then identify those people who can help you get it. Personally, I think trying to set superlong-term goals is ridiculous. Most people don't know what they're doing next weekend, let alone in five years.

However, you do need to have some sense of what you want to accomplish in the next year or so. For example, I am constantly trying to grow as a writer, so I set at least one large, intellectual challenge for myself per year.

Once you know what you want—it can be anything from a higher salary to more clients to a more creative or challenging job—you need to carefully single out those people who can help you get what you want.

Identify One or Two Things You Want in the Coming Year

In the real world, most of us can only work toward achieving one major goal at a time. Whether your goal is changing jobs, advancing at work, or carving out more free time, you have to be clear about what you want before you can focus on who can help you get it.

Soul-searching is needed before you begin. If you're looking for a new job, what would you like to do at a new job that your current employer isn't letting you do now? What's the next logical step in your career? A greater management role? An environment where your qualities will be better appreciated? Working with leaders who are more charismatic? Or companies that take bigger risks?

If you're looking for more responsibility where you work now, what would you want to do and what wouldn't you want to do? Is the extra work worth the extra money? How much more money would you want? If more money is the issue, is it better for you to do freelance work outside of your current job?

If you want to make good luck happen, you have to write down what you want. The art of making luck involves asking yourself a series of candid questions and committing yourself to your goals. You can't create good luck for yourself unless you have a fair idea of what you're trying to achieve.

Identify Your Gatekeepers of Opportunity

A gatekeeper of opportunity is someone with whom you are remotely friendly and who is plugged into a network of people you'd probably like to meet. This person can make your life luckier, but will do so only if you are able to show that you are worthy of the opportunities and that you'll know what to do with them once they're given to you.

Think about the people you know who can invite you to parties or introduce you to other key people. These are the people with whom you want to keep in close written and verbal contact. Think of them as red embers in a fireplace. Those embers need to be turned from time to time. If you neglect them, the fire dies.

Keeping in contact with prize sources shouldn't be misinterpreted as sucking up. Many people resist contacting key people who can help them out of fear that they will look as if they are begging for favors. Get over it. Luck, success, and happiness require open lines of communication that work both ways. Luck's gatekeepers understand that this is the way the world works and are usually happy to help—if you create the right impression.

Steps to setting up your luck network . . .

• **Assemble a dream team.** Go through your Rolodex and note every influential person in your chosen field with whom you are remotely friendly. List their names, as well as their fax and phone numbers, in a notebook. Jot down anyone who seems appropriate— even people you haven't spoken to in a while. Many big breaks come from the least likely contacts.

• **Indicate which people you plan to call and which ones you will fax.** The rule of thumb is to call only if you've spoken with or have seen the person within the past three months. Fax or send correspondence through the mail to everyone else before you call.

• **Create a separate file in your computer for each contact.** It's always better to lay the groundwork before you begin. The key to keeping up with your sources and the people they suggest you call is to be highly organized. Once the names start pouring in, you're going to need a system so that you can not only contact new people but also thank the person who gave you the referral. If you forget to express your gratitude, you won't likely get help from that person again.

Set up a file in your computer with your letterhead for each gate-keeper you plan to contact. Enter the fax number here too, so that when you're ready to write and print out the letter, it's all ready to go.

Know How to Ask for What You Want

Since you'll be faxing letters to most of the people on your hot list, your letter needs to bring them up to speed about you, give a sense of what you want, and in some cases invite them to lunch. Most people will be happy to help you, but only if you are brief and respectful in your correspondence.

Letter-writing secrets of lucky people . . .

• **Open your letter with a sincere compliment.** Everyone likes to have their good work acknowledged, and that goes double for luck's gatekeepers.

• **Keep your tone upbeat and exciting.** Remember, the purpose of the letter is to remind the gatekeeper of you and convey the impression that you're happy and excited about what you're doing. Never write about bad news, which will just make key contacts recoil and resist sharing opportunities with you.

• **Your last line should suggest a meeting—hint that it would be great to catch up.** Breakfast or lunch is ideal, because the setting is most conducive to creating a lucky impression. If the person is impressed, you're likely to get more opportunities than you had hoped for.

However, you shouldn't expect the person to offer you an opportunity immediately, nor should you ask for it. Instead, shoot for a smaller goal—getting the person to give you the names of a few contacts who could be instrumental in helping you. When those contacts help you out, be sure to let your gatekeeper know about it. Once a gatekeeper hears that a contact he or she gave you was incredibly helpful, you will probably be offered other names or additional assistance.

Strategies for Popping the Question

Most people who are meeting with a contact over lunch make the mistake of asking for help too soon. You're always much better off using most of your time together with your contact to bond and promote the great things you have been doing. Lunch is a fine art, and to do it effectively you need to give your relationship a chance to warm up.

When is the best time to ask for the names of people who can improve your luck? After you order coffee or, in other cases, it may be better to ask a day later, over the phone. The strategy here is to give yourself enough time to create the impression that you're lucky, that everything is going well, and that your request is only to make you luckier, not to pull you out of a jam.

Sometimes, by putting your gatekeeper on the spot too soon, your plan can backfire as the person worries why you seem so rushed and panicky. When in doubt, sit back and relax. Your only goal is to leave the person with a great impression of you.

Other secrets of people who always get what
they want at lunch . . .

• **Talk about the other person, not about yourself.** Once you've told your gatekeeper what you've been up to, steer the conversation back to them and keep it there. Let the person talk. Just listen—carefully—or ask great questions. Remember the lucky conversationalist's cardinal rule: People who don't talk are always considered great conversationalists.

• **Ask your gatekeepers how they handle tricky problems.**
When we are asked for advice, we immediately feel flattered. It feels good
to be recognized as an expert and to know that someone is interested
enough in us to seek our wisdom and problem-solving techniques. By
asking these types of questions, you will put your gatekeeper in a
mentor role—a dynamic that will prepare the gatekeeper for your
request for contacts and assistance.

• **Ask for help when you're asked how you're doing.** This question usually comes up toward the end of the meal, when you've both
relaxed. When a gatekeeper asks, "So, what else are you doing these
days?" it's the perfect lead-in for you to lay out your goal and ask for
the names of a few people who might know other people who can
help. By stating that you're looking for help two levels removed from
the gatekeeper, you've improved your chances of getting more of what
you want. By asking for leads from people your gatekeeper knows,
there's less risk that your gatekeeper will be embarrased if you screw
up or fail to impress.

Sounding Lucky on the Phone

The best time to reach key people is early in the morning, before the
day kicks in. Many people answer their own phones at that hour and
are more receptive to listening to you and giving you what you want. If
you wait until later to contact key people, you will probably reach
their voice mail or their assistants.

To sound lucky, you have to come across as confident. But you
also have to talk slowly. Many people make the mistake of talking too
quickly, usually out of nervousness. It's hard to be receptive to people
who talk quickly. Not only is it hard to follow what they are saying,
but we tend to equate fast-talkers with schemers and hucksters. To
seem confident and lucky over the phone, you need to slow down

what you're saying. Zig Ziglar, one of the country's top motivational speakers, suggests that people practice talking slower when talking to friends on the phone. If you can talk at a calm, easy pace, more of what you're trying to get across will get through.

Putting the "Power of Twos" in Motion

This is a technique that I've often used to create a great many opportunities fast. Once your gatekeeper gives you the names of two or more people to call, set out to get at least two names from each of them. Then you get two more from those contacts, and so on. Once you have a list of at least twenty new names and phone numbers, call each of them and ask for a meeting or lunch. You just need to be sure that you've thanked each contact appropriately as you move forward. Otherwise, you've left a bad impression—which can cause you bad luck.

Whether or not these new contacts choose to help you, and how much time and effort they give you, depends on how well you are able to project a lucky image. Remember, luck loves lucky people, and the quality of your opportunities depend chiefly on how lucky you seem to key people who are meeting you for the first time.

Make Time for Great Timing

How much good luck you eventually make for yourself depends on your ability to control the clock. If you are constantly tied up and unavailable to meet with key people, you won't be able to learn from those experiences or receive information that could help you. If you can't return phone calls, keep up with important office issues, or get out for business lunches, fewer opportunities will come your way. And most of those that do come your way will slide by unnoticed.

Luck and time are related. People who always have one eye on their opportunities and another on their wristwatch free themselves to create and follow up on opportunities. You can't be lucky if you are always at your desk. You may get promoted eventually, but it likely will be long after the luckier people who were able to get around the office, talk to colleagues, and attend meetings.

A person I know who has had three jobs with increasingly higher salaries over the past five years lunches at restaurants every day from 12:30 to 3:00 P.M. People who know her have always wondered how she was able to eat for so long and get everything done. Doesn't she have to involve herself with the nitty-gritty? Doesn't she have to write memos, badger her staff, and solve everyday office problems? How does that kind of marathon lunch schedule allow her to do that?

When I asked her, this savvy executive said that not only does she hire great people specifically to absorb the mundane aspects of her job, but she also delegates responsibility and backs off, weighing in only at the last minute, and then only to fine-tune. When the work isn't up to her standards, she's tough on her top managers.

"My job is not to make every person on my staff a superstar. Those who are exceptional will rise. I just need enough smart managers in place to let me get out of the office and generate business contacts and absorb new ideas and solutions." What about all the phone calls that keep the rest of us tied down? "I only return the ones I can, and I never return a call immediately. Fast replies mean instant access. I don't want people thinking that they have that. That's why I do most of my less important call-backs between 3:00 and 4:00 P.M., when most people are in meetings. What's important is freeing up my time to be visible both in the office and outside of the office."

Don't get the wrong impression about this woman. Those lunches aren't about eating. They produce contacts for her, generate new ideas, and give her tremendous exposure in her field. By being out so often, she is considered lucky by almost everyone who knows her, because she can pull it off. "My job is to be outside representing my company. My image is the company's image. I can't afford *not* to look lucky, and my company can't afford for me to look *unlucky* either."

Here's how this lucky executive suggests making the most of available time . . .

• **Simplify everything you do.** Throw out or pass along tasks that eat up your creative-thinking time or time needed to gain visibility.

• **Throw out almost everything after you read it.** Everything is replaceable.

• **Set specific dates and times for meetings for the entire year so that you can free up time for key interactions with outside sources.**

• **Show your staff how to deal with crises, and then let them solve them.** Hire smart people to do what you don't want to worry about. Look for people who are precise, detail-oriented, and highly responsible.

If you are not in a position to hire people to absorb some of your daily workload, focus on what you love to do most and consciously avoid taking on responsibilities and projects that will distract you. Many people who want to succeed make the mistake of trying to do everything well. You stand a much better chance of making luck if you continuously polish your strengths and forget about your weaknesses— unless, of course, they relate to what you love to do most.

Remember, you'll never be great at everything. By no longer bothering with your weaknesses, you will create blocks of time that can be used to think of your next move and set up new opportunities.

Take the Time Test

Most people think they are efficient. But you need to assess how efficient you really are so you can keep menial tasks from tying you down. Then, when good fortune looms, you will have time to explore the opportunity.

Questions to ask yourself to assess whether you have plenty
of time to make good luck happen . . .

• **What's on your desk right now?** If there are more than two stacks of papers there, you're doing something wrong.

Solution: Divide your work into two stacks. The one on the right is work that needs to be addressed that day. The one on the left is personal issues such as following up on insurance claims, calling the cable company, finding a plumber, and so on. Everything else should be filed away or tossed out.

• **What's most important in those stacks?** Are there any surprises as you work your way through the stacks—like projects or paperwork that should have been addressed or answered days ago?

Solution: Organize your stacks before you leave each night so that the most pressing item is on top.

• **What are you doing the day after tomorrow?** If you don't know, you're not on top of your schedule.

Solution: Simplify your life. Most people struggle with fancy technological gadgets to track their schedules. Or they use complicated, three-ring, leather date books to keep track of their appointments.

I know exactly what my schedule is each week and never miss a meeting. I use a month-at-a-glance planner that costs $11.95 and weighs next to nothing. It has a flexible cover and slips easily into my bag. I review it at night and when I arrive at work, scanning not only that day's meetings and obligations but also the days ahead.

• **How long do you plan to spend on the things you need to do?** Some people get bogged down on the tasks they need to complete. As a result, they may only tackle two rather than the five tasks on their agenda.

Solution: I slot my day in thirty-minute blocks. If something takes more than thirty minutes, I put it aside until the next day. It's far better to make headway on five items than complete only one.

• **Do you really need all that junk?** I'm amazed when I walk into someone's office and it looks like a used-book store. Lots of books and knickknacks mean clutter, confusion, and misplaced papers. You can't be lucky if you're a mess.

Solution: If you haven't referred to a book in the past year, get rid of it. The books that remain on your shelf should be kept neat and orderly. Toss or file all papers that you haven't looked at in a week. You don't need them—or you can access them again later if necessary. You also don't need all that junk on your desk and bulletin board. Minimize anything that causes mental disorder and confusion.

• **At what hour do you return calls each day?** If you call people back at all times during the day, you will never get anything done.

Solution: The best time to return calls is in the afternoon, because your mornings should be devoted to brain work. I deal with about fifty freelance writers, and I'm also at the receiving end of dozens of calls from public relations people, book editors, and experts who appear regularly in my newsletter or would like to. I return almost all of my nonpressing calls one to two days later. I don't like to be too available, unless it's an emergency. By making myself scarce, people only call me if it's important.

Your Office Must Look Lucky

A crisp office is important for two reasons: First, if you're organized, you're working efficiently, and efficiency is the key to taking control of your time and generating more luck. Second, a clean office makes the people who come to see you feel good. A messy office reduces their respect for you and your work.

Try to think of your work space as if it were a hospital operating room—sterile, orderly, and smart. In today's technology-crazed office where information, paperwork, and projects can easily clutter all available space, your area must look organized and efficient. Otherwise, the resulting mess will make it look as if you're working too hard or not smart enough. Arrange books neatly on the shelf, making sure they line up at the edge. Fill each shelf wall-to-wall, with no gaps or tilted books. Your desk should look neatly arranged when you leave each night. Anytime you leave your office, reorganize the stacks of papers on your desk. Your luck depends on it.

Managing Incoming Work and Distractions

Never before has there been such a struggle to keep up with tasks that have to be done. Prioritize all the work that lands in your in-box as soon as possible. Anything that comes in should get answered and distributed immediately and without delay. If it requires time, take it home or make five minutes for it.

Distractions are also the enemies of lucky people. If you can't get your work done, you won't be free to create and take advantage of opportunities. Someone I know stands while working the phones at his desk in the afternoons—to keep people out of his office. Other people put paperwork on their guest chairs to discourage visitors from popping by. When lucky people are interrupted, they set a mental time limit or avoid looking up from their work. Still other lucky people walk out of their offices when people walk in. "I seek out the people I need to see," says a mutual fund manager I know. "If I am interrupted by someone, I imagine that person as a hot potato. I juggle the person and toss him or her out as soon as possible."

PART TWO

THE 7 SECRETS OF LUCKY PEOPLE

Opportunity doesn't knock.
You knock and opportunity answers.

Anonymous

How do some people manage to attract so many great opportunities so frequently? We know that lucky people think of themselves as lucky and actively seek out people who can help them get what they want. But believing you're lucky, getting close to people who hold opportunities and managing your time doesn't automatically make you lucky.

What sets truly lucky people apart is their behavior. Lucky people act in ways that compel others to help them. Their special behavior convinces key people that they're worthy of opportunities and that they'll know what to do with those opportunities once they get them.

All of the lucky people I have studied behave in similar ways that make them ideal candidates for lucky breaks. Their luck-generating behavior can be divided into seven different strategies. All you need to do is to master one or two of these behavior skills to become lucky. The behavior should eventually feel natural to you, in much the same way a dancer knows instinctively how many steps to take during a performance or a baseball infielder knows reflexively where to throw the ball when a grounder comes his way.

While each of the seven luck-making behavior skills is distinct, they all have one thing in common: When executed perfectly, each will cause you to stand out in a positive way and be remembered by people who can offer you golden opportunities. The more convincing you are, the easier your life will become because a greater number of unexpected, beneficial opportunities will present themselves.

Remember, most teriffic opportunities do not fall into our laps. They are seduced there. Start practicing the following strategies, and your luck will improve almost immediately.

■ CHAPTER SIX ■

LUCKY SECRET 1:
Make Life Look Easy—But Don't Rub It In

If hard work is the key to success,
I'd rather pick the lock.

HENNY YOUNGMAN

America is probably the only country in the world where people who make difficult things look effortless are admired and rewarded. In other cultures, only royalty and the jet set are entitled to exhibit a laid-back approach to life's challenges. Everyone else is expected to work hard and show it. In America, however, we revere those who work hard and hide it.

This attitude is most evident in how we view professional athletes and entertainers. We are amazed when a Major League baseball pitcher throws a perfect game and never shows the strain or struggle of his effort. We love the quarterback who completes pass after pass in the final moments of a Super Bowl and then runs in the winning touchdown on a draw play. Muhammad Ali was a brilliant boxer and arguably the best athlete of the twentieth century. But he is universally loved not because he trained hard or fought grueling battles but because he was a champ who made boxing look easy. He made us feel we all could float and sting for fifteen rounds without becoming exhausted.

Our admiration for people who do hard things effortlessly extends to everyday situations as well. We respect the person at work who skillfully manages fifty people without showing strain. We admire the friend who always seems to find great jobs without spending much time at it. We respect these people because we know that what they have accomplished is hard, but we idolize them because they keep the stress and sweat of their efforts hidden. We all know people who are good at what they do but whose efforts look like a struggle. We respect them, but we don't root for them.

Struggling isn't what the new American Dream is all about. We want the people we admire to confirm our belief that fame and fortune are easily attainable. People who struggle and show how hard they're working don't make us feel good. They force us to share their angst. The goal is to get what will make you comfortable and happy without killing yourself in the process.

To be successful, you must be good at what you do. But to be lucky, you need charm. Stage actors who sail through performances receive the most applause. Their delivery may be imperfect, but if their attitude is right, the audience will always be on their side. I saw Whoopi Goldberg on her final night in Broadway's *A Funny Thing Happened on the Way to the Forum*. Despite making several big mistakes that were obvious to everyone there, she brought down the house by laughing them off. She was enjoying herself, despite her lack of Broadway experience. Had Goldberg become angry, frustrated, or embarrassed by her limitations, she would have lost the audience's adoration and respect.

By making life look hard, you create an emotional chasm that is tough for an audience to bridge. Broadway actress and singer Rebecca

Luker, whose performance in *Showboat* was nominated for a Tony and who was Maria in *The Sound of Music,* told me backstage that she considers winning over audiences just as important as delivering a great performance. "Some nights you can feel the hostility out there—either because people have had a long week, or the seats are uncomfortable, or they're just in a bad mood," Luker said. "I have to sense this hostility and work harder to charm them and win them over. It's not a matter of singing louder or running faster across the stage. I need to convey that I'm having the greatest time playing Maria. When I do, they always come around."

Laugh Off Life's Ambushes

To get what you want, you have to meet deadlines, be responsible, produce high-quality work, and take risks. Along the way, you experience disappointment, rejection, and failure. Such setbacks are nerve-wracking. It's human nature to feel angry and humiliated when you screw up or when things don't turn out as you had hoped. No one likes to be reminded of his or her shortcomings.

Yet some people seem to laugh off life's ambushes. They are serious about their work, but they never seem too seriously affected by setbacks—at least not outwardly. Sure they feel disappointed and ashamed. But the length of time those feelings paralyze them is relatively short. When you can take life's hardest shots without flinching, you make life look easy. And when you make life look easy, people think you are lucky. When you are lucky, you are someone people want to see succeed.

Why do people who make life look easy seem lucky? Because most of us secretly believe that we are schlubs at the core. We are a bundle of insecurities and self-doubt. We all suffer to some extent from the impostor syndrome—the secret belief that we aren't quite qualified enough to do what we're paid to do. We fear that sooner or later our charade is going to be discovered and exposed. Every beautiful fashion model thinks she is flawed or less beautiful than another model. Every great musician wishes he or she played like someone else. The biggest movie stars are riddled with insecurities.

From time to time, everyone questions the quality of their talents and skills. We all have fears and weaknesses, or some vulnerability that we carry from childhood and spend our lifetimes concealing. No matter how successful we become, many of us believe we don't really deserve what we have accomplished. That's why we respect people who seem completely at ease and impervious to mistakes, insults, and failure.

By learning to shrug off emotional assaults, you will come across as fearless. You will make others believe you have special powers. You will also make people who hold opportunities more likely to offer them to you. Part of the art of making life look easy is the ability to control nervousness and self-doubt—the archenemies of good fortune. When you seem nervous, you undermine other people's confidence in you. When you exhibit self-doubt, you no longer seem in control. People will instinctively pull away from you.

One of the most relaxed people I know is Matt Lauer, cohost of NBC's *Today* show. His easygoing, casual manner makes us believe he feels completely at ease interviewing the most intimidating celebrities and politicians. His ratings are high because he's intelligent, viewers feel comfortable with him, and because he makes what he does look so easy.

Here are his secrets of staying relaxed—
even in high-tension situations . . .

• **Prepare for situations that make you nervous.** "Whether it's Hillary Clinton or John Grisham, I'm never nervous about the interview process unless I haven't had adequate preparation the night before," Lauer says. "Careful preparation helps me gain control over the unknown, which is really what makes most people nervous or frightened. The more familiar I become with someone, the more at ease I become. But you can overprepare in this business, too. For example, you can try to memorize too much, which can cause you to forget everything you tried to remember. I stay relaxed by preparing just enough so that I can speak to guests knowledgeably and listen carefully. I'm more interested in creating a bond between us than impressing them."

• **Imagine that the people you're talking to for the first time are guests on your show.** "You can't give up control because of a mistake," Lauer says. "One of the reasons it's easy for me to be confident on the *Today* show is that it's my and Katie Couric's show. And that's exactly how we think of it. When people are guests on *your* show, you automatically feel more comfortable. They're on your turf, and they've come to see you. I imagine that the guests are in my living room, which immediately relaxes my mind and body language. Anyone can create this mindset in any situation."

• **Make believe your mistakes are only a five-second blip.** "In my business if I agonize over a mistake, I've already spent too much time thinking about it, and I'm probably going to make another mistake in my next interview," Lauer says. "You have to look at your mistakes the way viewers look at them on TV. What may seem like a five-minute disaster often is really a five-second blip in the minds of viewers. If you're still upset at yourself, remind yourself you're probably the only one who remembers the mistake or cares. You must constantly tell yourself that life isn't perfect, and neither are you.

"One way to avoid being bogged down by mistakes is never try to cover them up. If you make a mistake, have the guts to admit it. People can't blame you for making mistakes. They can only blame you for making the same mistake twice, and there's no better teacher than an embarrassing moment."

Drawing the Line Between Cocky and Lucky

When I think of the many lucky people I know who make life look easy, I realize that they rarely attribute their success to their own genius. In fact, they go out of their way to bring themselves down a few notches. That's why they are so well-liked. If they waltzed around telling people how easy life is, no one would want to help them.

Who wants to help people who insist they don't need it? Talking yourself up also makes you seem like an egomaniac, and the penalty for hubris is enormous. Hubris invites predators. You set yourself up to become a stationary target for people who want to see you fail. Rise too high and there will be plenty of people who will want to see you shot down. I've learned that people wish you well to a point. Then they actively wish for your failure. There's a point where you make life look so easy that you become a lightning rod for other people's inadequacies. That makes people look for your flaws.

Many talented and intelligent people I know who made their achievements look too easy missed out on great opportunities. They were smart, but they were too high on themselves and they intimidated or antagonized people who could have helped them. Their behavior triggered envy and resentment, not admiration.

The trick, therefore, is knowing where the line exists between confident and cocky. To make life look easy without rubbing it in, you must develop a strong sense of gratitude for what you have and an appreciation for what you don't have yet. Realizing that everything you have achieved can disappear will keep you from overinflating your self-worth and prevent you from rubbing your good fortune in the faces of those who can give you what you want or help you out of a jam.

Hang in There—and Give Serendipity a Chance

Matt Lauer says when making life look easy fails to produce the good luck you want, back off a little and let life take its course. While looking cool under fire improves your odds of attracting opportunity, there are going to be times when good fortune will elude you nonetheless. When you can't get what you want—even though you've tried everything possible—you have to take a break and let it be for a while. Instead of succumbing to discouragement and giving up on your dream, tell yourself that you *will* get what you want—it will just take a little longer.

"Just before getting my job at NBC, I couldn't make luck happen at all," Lauer recalls. "I couldn't make my career happen. I didn't know what was wrong. It was a very strange situation. Every time I was hired to host a show in different markets around the country, the response from people on the show was positive, but the ratings were poor. Six months later I'd get a pink slip. I was never quite right for the formats. On one show, I was too young. On another show, I was too aggressive. Then I was too urban. There was always something wrong.

"So when things really started to go badly in the late 1980s and early 1990s—when I lost five shows in a row—I retreated from the business. I was unemployed for a year and a half. I even had to give up my apartment in New York City because I couldn't afford the rent. I sat in my cottage in the suburbs and did a lot of self-evaluating while I waited for the phone to ring. When it did ring, the offers were bad and on the fringes of respectable television. My dwindling bank account eventually convinced me to look for work outside of television.

"One morning, as I was going to get my coffee and paper with my dog, I saw a tree-trimming truck on the side of the road with a "Help Wanted" sign in the window. I took down the number and called that morning. There was an answering machine, so I left my name and number. About three hours later the phone rang. I was all set to begin my career as a tree-trimmer, but on the other end was the secretary of the general manager of WNBC, the local station in New York City.

"She was calling to set up an interview. Management had seen a tape of my work and they wanted me to anchor the morning news. Talk about luck—the tape had come to the general manager from a meeting he had with someone else a year earlier. I didn't even know the job existed. A month later, I was back in front of a camera—in the country's top-rated market.

"My year-and-a-half wait for work was tough for me. I had gone from college to my first four jobs never applying for work. Everybody had always called *me* with job offers. In the beginning, opportunity landed in my lap. But then it fell right through my lap and left me with nothing. So when I went to work for WNBC in New York, I was happy to work both ends of the clock—the 6:00 A.M. show and the 5:00 P.M. *Live at Five* news. By working hard and staying relaxed, I was noticed by the *Today* show.

"My past experience taught me that everything can be taken away from you in a flash. One of the criticisms my friends level against me is that I never just enjoy what I've accomplished. I'd love to, but I'm the last person who feels that I've made it. My stepfather always had a saying: 'You're not a member of the workforce until you've had to look for a job.'

"There isn't a day that I get out of bed without really appreciating what's been done for me. I am very fortunate that I have a family that keeps me well-grounded. If I were ever to become a prima donna, they would slap me down so fast. I really like people, and my hard years only enhanced my respect for the hardships others face. As a result, I try to get along as well with the guy who pulls cables in our studio as I do with the senior producer of our show."

Avoiding the Ego Trap While Making Life Look Easy

If you can make what you do look easy and make people feel comfortable with your success, you will improve your odds of being thought of as lucky. The more relaxed you make people feel, the more they will gravitate toward you and want to give you what you want.

Here's how lucky people make life look easy without falling into the ego trap . . .

• **Get a kick out of being you.** Matt Lauer believes it's impossible to teach someone to act naturally. But you can make people relax by being honest about who you are and by not trying to be what you're not. That takes a great deal of confidence. But boosting your confidence is easier than it seems. Confidence isn't some special power you're given at birth. Self-confidence is merely the ability to identify your strengths and attributes and prevent criticism from shoving you too far away from what you're most comfortable doing.

Only when you are comfortable with yourself can you be confident in your skills and talents and ignore negative criticism. When you know you do good work, you instantly relax and make life look easy. However, if you suffer under the feedback and criticism you receive, you will begin to believe it. That's when you'll try to change who you are and become less confident in the process.

"About a week after I was offered the job at New York's WNBC," Matt Lauer says, "I called the station manager and news director and said, 'Look, before I start a month from now, would you guys like me to go to a media consultant? Would you like me to go to someone to learn the craft of news anchoring?' Their response was, 'Whoa, whoa, whoa, absolutely not. We're hiring you because you're not the traditional anchor. Don't change a thing. Don't even think about changing.

We want you to come in and be the guy on the demo tape we saw, not some guy you learn to be in an anchor session. Stay who you are. Your value will be recognized.'"

• **Make people feel great.** If you can make people feel great about themselves and about meeting you, they're going to want to help you. Making people feel great can include doing something as simple as asking how they feel or praising them. You constantly have to ask yourself what kind of impact you're having on people and recognize that the more positive you make others feel, the more confident and relaxed you will seem.

If you think back on all of the golden opportunities that have recieved, you'll realize that most seemed to have come by accident. But, in reality, most of your opportunities came from people behind the scenes who thought highly of you and recommended you. Chances are that you made those people feel great in some way.

• **Look better and act dumber than your competition.** "To make life look easy, you have to wear great clothes without overdoing it," says Michael Stolper, one of the country's top money managers who represents many wealthy, successful clients. "Then, once you look as if everything you touch turns to gold, you'll have to tone down that image. I know how fortunate I've been and how lucky I seem. So when I'm speaking in front of an audience, I'll start by saying something like, 'The great thing about this business is that someone with my IQ can make a living at it,' or, 'I'm just a working stiff who got lucky.' When you're self-deprecating, you bring people close and make it possible for them to believe they can do what you did.

"On one level, people want to believe that you inherited all your money or stumbled across your good fortune. If you're wealthy or successful, they want to believe that you are an aristocrat, which explains away how you get so much of what you want. There's a small problem though. No one wants to help an aristocrat. Aristocrats are self-sufficient. But if you're self-deprecating, you're admitting that you have the same fears as everyone else. Putting yourself down or laughing at yourself hurts, but the long-term payoff for your image and your luck is great."

• **Become known for being loyal to your friends.** When you develop a reputation for sticking by your friends, you win the respect of important people. Being known as a loyal friend shows that you stand by those who help you and that you know how to reciprocate when a favor is done for you. As a result, you make life look easy and you become someone people want to help.

A willingness to stand by your friends also shows that you're willing to get your hands dirty. No matter how easy your life may seem, if you are known as someone who sacrifices and supports your friends, you show that you're interested in more than just your own success and ego gratification. When it's clear you're willing to go to bat for people you care about, others will line up to gain membership in this elite club.

Loyalty to friends can be expressed in several subtle ways. The lucky people I know never bad-mouth their friends. They never back out of helping them, provided the request for help is within reason. And they always support their friends. The only stipulation they have is that the person they help be equally supportive.

• **Develop a reputation for telling it like it is.** The more powerful people become, the harder it is for them to find others who will tell them the truth. They are surrounded by "yes" men who tell them only what they want to hear. If you are assertive and aren't afraid to speak openly, the powerful will reward you for having the courage to do what most others are afraid to do in their presence—speak boldly. But being honest entails great risk. You never know how your remarks will be interpreted or what the reaction will be. After all, killing the messenger is an age-old sport. Be honest, be candid, but also be gentle. Luck is the art of being simultaneously fearless and respectful of another's feelings.

I know a senior executive who makes an extra $100,000 a year just being a director on boards of companies. He holds those positions because he is known for telling people what he thinks. Much of his job in that capacity, he says, involves showing up for an hour a month—with a fair amount of basic small talk, a little weather talk, some sports talk, and occasionally a decision. Sure he's smart, but those board opportunities were presented to him because people value his honesty and fidelity. Otherwise his participation would be worthless.

Telling powerful people how you feel is relatively easy, provided that what you say is positioned so it isn't insulting. To become known for your honesty, you must be able to say what other people are afraid to say. As you become known for your truthfulness, more people at higher levels will want to help you.

• **Drive stakes through your "cosmic vampires."** You won't be able to make life look easy if most of the people you know are making life hard for you. You have to make a conscious effort to surround yourself with people who reduce the amount of stress and strain in your life, so that you can concentrate on making good luck happen.

"I only know lucky people because I avoid negative people at all costs," Michael Stolper says. "I prefer positive people out of a primitive feeling that negative people are just going to screw me up. The big problem with negative behavior is that it's infectious. It gets you thinking that way.

"There are some people whom I call 'cosmic vampires.' They love to create negative energy and a negative environment that eliminates all positive thinking. To make your life look easy, you have to eliminate these people from your life. These people cannot be finessed. They have to be removed as decisively and as quickly as possible. If I don't want to be someplace because of somebody else, then they have control over my life. That's unacceptable."

Stolper suggests making a serious effort to seek people who think positively and to limit your association with people who see themselves as victims or who are clearly envious of you. Your outlook will improve and you will be better able to make life look easy.

• **Think of confrontational people as irate customers rather than adversaries.** People who make life look easy never let the hostility or envy of others affect them. To keep themselves from slipping into that trap, they view the negative people they must deal with as difficult customers. When you are faced with a customer who is upset, you never take their anger personally. Instead, you find ways to get them out of the way as fast as possible.

"Negative people you can't avoid are often those with whom you work or do business," Stolper says. "Unless they leave your department or change occupations, you're stuck with them. But if you treat them as adversaries, you'll take their attacks personally and spend far too much energy trying to change a relationship that can't be changed.

"Instead, try treating confrontational people like hostile customers. Your fuse is a lot longer and you can put distance between you and your temper. The cooler you remain, the more easygoing you seem. The more easygoing you seem, the easier life will be for you."

■CHAPTER SEVEN■

LUCKY SECRET 2:
Cultivate Charisma—Even if You're Shy

A great person shows greatness by the way
he or she treats little people.

THOMAS CARLYLE

Most people do not think of themselves as charismatic, and those who do would never admit it publicly. Charisma is a powerful and scary quality that we think other people possess, but not us. We think of charisma as the ability to cast spells over people and make them like you. It is also universally assumed that charisma is a trait you're born with, like hair color or height.

The truth is that anyone can consciously work to make their personality much more appealing. By boosting your magnetism, you will become more likable and more people will want to offer you opportunities. The right level of charisma will charm the right people who can improve your fortune within a very short period of time.

What Is Charisma?

Charisma began as *charis*, an ancient Greek noun meaning a spiritual favor or gift. The gift was believed to be granted by God to people as a token of grace, and it was originally exemplified by the power to heal and the gift of tongues. The word first appeared in print in Greek translations of the New Testament, and entered the English language in 1641 when studies of civilization and ancient Greece were revived in the wake of the Reformation.

The first secular use of the word *charisma* was used by the German sociologist Max Weber in 1922. It appears in his writings about the leadership qualities that capture the imagination of the masses and inspire unswerving allegiance and devotion.

Not much has changed in several thousand years. We are still in awe of charismatic people because of their seemingly magical powers of attraction. All charismatic people have a compelling personality that satisfies our need to be recognized and motivated. They also satisfy our need to be led and to follow. We gravitate to strong people for leadership. But charisma as we know it today goes way beyond leadership. After all, you can be an effective leader but not be charismatic. Or you can be a good administrator with great ideas, but still not be very inspiring.

To be considered charismatic, you now need to possess an ability to put people at ease and draw them close. Most modern presidents have been charismatic. They have been able to capture the public's imagination and have inspired unwavering devotion. As we know, Ronald Reagan was particularly charismatic. He had a sweetness and benign quality that made him extremely difficult to resist. Even his son, Ron Reagan Jr., whose relationship with his father was widely reported to be rocky at best, has said that the senior Reagan was pretty tough to turn down when he "turned on the high beams." His charisma was effortless—a striking combination of cinematic good looks, a luminous smile, an uncanny ability to make people who came in contact with him feel good, and a powerful way of carrying himself.

Why do we find charismatic people so appealing? Our exposure to charisma and its powers of attraction and devotion probably started in high school. In high school, most of us weren't the centers of attention. That honor often went to members of the varsity club and the cheerleading squad. We envied their power and wished we were friends with them. The reality is that most of us never got very close to them or anyone else who was the center of attention. So when we meet someone today who is charismatic and outgoing, they make us feel special and we feel energized—we are finally being accepted by the cool kids.

But charisma comes in varying shades of intensity, and there's a big difference between just being a great salesperson and being charismatic. For someone to be truly charismatic in the broadest sense, he or she has to believe in what they're saying and make you believe that they are genuinely sincere. Charismatic people get what they want because people feel compelled to give it to them. They make other people feel as if they are part of the inner circle. By projecting warmth to those with whom they come in contact, charismatic people validate the ideas and opinions of others.

The Charisma-Luck Connection

Charisma provides a sensation not unlike that of a beautiful room in which the furniture and fabrics are so pleasing that we're compelled to sit down. Charismatic people exude a spiritual and physical symmetry that makes it impossible not to be captivated or accommodating. We want to give charismatic people what they want because we hope that some of their powers will rub off on us.

Giving charismatic people what they want makes them happy, and making charismatic people happy is the best way to make them acknowledge our existence, if only briefly. Charisma is associated with luck because both seem to come through divine power. We are always searching for superheroes we can support. The hope is that through our association with these superheroes, we will be able to learn their secrets, become just like them, and have others adore us.

People with high levels of personal magnetism attract a huge number of opportunities because their body language asks for it. "I once had a dance teacher at Smith College who walked into the room with her shoulders hunched over," says Sally Quinn, the Washington, D.C., socialite who has met hundreds of charismatic people over the years as a reporter for the *Washington Post* and as the wife of the newspaper's former editor, Ben Bradlee. "This teacher's head would be down, her stomach would be sticking out, and her feet would be splayed. Then she'd say, 'What message am I sending you?' When no one answered, she said, 'I'm apologizing for my existence.'

"Then she'd leave the room and return walking briskly with her head held high, her shoulders and neck and back straight, and her chest forward. She'd ask, 'What message am I sending you now? I'm saying that I'm confident and feel good about myself. I'm happy to be here and I'm a worthwhile human being.' That was a very valuable lesson, and I've seen it in action hundreds of times over the years. Charismatic people get more of what they want because they carry themselves like winners. When they walk into a room, people say, 'Gosh, that person must be terrific because they act as though they're terrific. I want that person to be on my team, to work in my office, to be in my life.'"

Another reason why charisma generates so much opportunity is that there is an "expected" quality about it. When you are dynamic, you send a signal that says, "I expect to be well-liked, I expect to get ahead, I expect to be hired for this job, or I expect to be successful." If you expect opportunity, most people you meet will say to themselves, "Sure, why not?" Charismatic people also make us feel confident that they will appreciate and make the most of whatever assistance we provide them.

If you are perceived as charismatic, people are more likely to make a greater effort for you and you're more likely to have successful outcomes. Charisma makes you look lucky, which in turn attracts golden opportunities.

Secrets of Charismatic People

We equate charisma with luck because we assume that charismatic people were born with the powers that make them likable. But charisma isn't genetic. Charisma can be acquired at any time in life, and even a *little* charisma goes a long way.

Charismatic people do very specific things to make themselves appealing and win the loyalty of people they meet. Those skills either come naturally because they were developed at an early age, or they are learned and practiced. While most people will never have Ronald Reagan's natural sincerity or Helen Hunt's aw-shucks charm, you *can* be more charismatic than you are now and make yourself more appealing.

The secret is to look at what makes charismatic people tick, and focus on learning and practicing those qualities until you are comfortable with them. Even if you aren't naturally dynamic, you can do a pretty good impression of someone who is charismatic by combining enthusiasm and humility. A high level of energy will make people take notice, while your humility will make you accessible and likable.

This combination is important, because either behavior without the other can negatively affect your luck. A high level of energy can make you seem hyperactive or even reckless. Humility by itself can make you seem wimpy. Combine the two, however, and you will make people respect you *and* want to help you.

But take it slow. Experts in charisma say it usually takes six months to a year to sift new behavior into your personality without alerting the people who know you. "Charisma is a lot like those hair-color products," says Andrew DuBrin, a business professor at Rochester Institute of Technology and a charisma expert. "You need to change in small steps. To be convincing, you can't go from gray on Friday to black on Monday. Becoming even a little more charismatic should be a gradual transformation process. Otherwise, your new personality won't seem natural. By definition, charisma must seem effortless."

Charisma is in the details. To create a reputation for being charismatic, you have to connect with people and impress them so greatly that they can't wait to help you and spread the word about you.

Here's how charismatic people intensify every encounter and develop a more dynamic personality and reputation . . .

• **Thrust and squeeze.** The bonding power of a firm handshake dates back thousands of years. It has always signified trust and strength. Your handshake is the gateway to your personality and power. Every charismatic person I know has a firm handshake, and they all rank it high among those things that leave a lasting impression.

But not everyone has a large hand or a strong grip. This is especially true of women. A foolproof strategy suggested by a charismatic person I know is to pull your arm back slightly and thrust your hand into the other person's hand. The thrust ensures solid and complete contact. It also protects against your hand winding up in an awkward or weak position. And it makes a subtle statement about your energy and enthusiasm. If you apply a squeeze immediately after connecting, your handshake will come off as a firm hug, and everyone likes those.

• **See eye to eye.** Charismatic people make eye contact and are able to hold it without looking away. This is not as easy as it seems, since most people close their eyes or look away as they speak. Eye contact says you are truly interested in the other person and that you are accessible. Even in a crowded room, the other person has to feel as if the relationship is personal.

Many people have trouble holding eye contact. Some can't think about what they are about to say without looking away. Others get self-conscious and look away as soon as the person looks back. Still others feel they are making the other person uncomfortable.

If you watch tapes of Ronald Reagan, you'll notice that his strategy was to look down and press his lips together while the other person was talking. Then he'd look up just as the other person was finishing and look right into that person's eyes, as if to say, "I understand exactly, and I agree with you." When he responded, he looked directly into the eyes of the other person and into the eyes of those standing to the immediate left and right of the person. This kept the person from feeling uncomfortable and also made others feel part of the conversation.

The eye-to-eye strategies used by Reagan and other charismatic people do not come easy. If you aren't used to public speaking or meeting people at parties, using your eyes strategically to charm others can be learned if you consciously make an effort to do so and practice every chance you get.

• **Remember their names—and the names of their kids.** Charismatic people are absolutely brilliant at remembering names. They do it by immediately saying the person's name and linking it to some famous person or an object. So a Paul may become Paul McCartney or a Sharon becomes Sharon Stone. The key is to immediately begin drilling the person's name into your head. Once you get this technique down, you'll avoid those embarrassing name-forgetting situations that undercut the smoothness of your presentation and ruin your ability to make a clean, charismatic impression.

• **Express your emotions.** You'll never be considered charismatic if you are reserved. You have to be excited about everything you're talking about and express yourself colorfully. Analogies and hand gestures leave big impressions, because the people you meet are more likely to remember what you've said. Force yourself to talk in ways that are highly positive and expressive. You want to be thought of as motivating and inspiring. If you're open about how you feel and you're enthusiastic, people will find you appealing.

People who are charismatic stand out because they express their feelings about timely issues, whether they are talking about the news, the movies, or just people. A good place to look for timely material is in newspapers and magazines. Read all of the way through articles for the material most people miss, or tie together news events that relate to each other. Come up with an overarching theme that people may not have put together yet. The greater your excitement and openness, the more likely you will be thought of as charismatic.

• **Smile broadly and laugh lustily.** We love people who make us laugh. Laughing feels good, and people who are funny are automatically more attractive to us. Just think of your favorite comedians. Everyone secretly wishes they were wittier, because to be witty is to be funny and smart and to have a positive influence on people.

Nearly all witty people are extremely well-read and knowledgeable about many different subjects. "A great sense of humor and honesty are a killer combination when it comes to charisma," says Sally Quinn.

• **Imagine that you're an electric generator.** One of the most important aspects of charismatic people is a high level of energy. "That's what Jack Kennedy had," Sally Quinn says. "All of the Kennedys have a lot of energy. When you meet them, it's as if an engine is running. Whenever someone charismatic enters a room, there's almost an audible hum. When you meet them, it feels like there's an electrical current running between you and them."

People with a high level of energy know the importance of being energetic. They are pumped up, and we admire their vigor. Vitality implies youth and sexual stamina, both of which imply long life.

• **Humanize what you have to say.** All charismatic people enter a room as if they're the center of the world but spend most of their time focusing on others. The key to charisma is making *other* people feel special. One of the most effective ways to do that is by putting other people's needs before your own. Charisma isn't about selling yourself. It's about making other people feel special. When you give other people a chance to talk, you become a great listener. When you give people a chance to feel great about themselves, you become charismatic. It's that simple.

Strategies for making other people feel great . . .

• **Personalize your compliments.** When you praise people, you risk sounding insincere if your comments are too broad. If you say, "Nice job this week," you sound as if you are looking for praise in kind. But if you say, "Nice job on that report—your conclusion was perfectly put," the compliment is specific and immediately more sincere.

The point here isn't to hand out praise just to improve your ratings with other people. However, when you do have something nice to say, look for something in particular about the person or their accomplishments to praise. It will have much more impact, and your intentions will be better appreciated.

- **Be sensitive about other people's insecurities.** When you praise people, realize that your compliments may cause them to withdraw. Read their body language and their reactions carefully and be sensitive about their insecurities. In some cases, your praise may be more effective when you're one-on-one rather than in a group.

- **Get over being shy.** "I don't have a lot of patience for people who claim to be shy," says Sally Quinn. "Often that just means they're self-involved, that they're just thinking, 'Me, me, me—what about me? What are they thinking about me? How are they reacting to me?' rather than, 'Let me think about *them* for a minute.'"

How can you overcome shyness? When you walk into a room, instead of thinking, "What do they think about me?" say to yourself, "What do I think about them? Let me go and ask them how they're doing. How are they feeling? What's going on with them?" By putting the emphasis on the people you are about to meet, you will immediately begin thinking of questions to ask rather than being hamstrung by your own self-consciousness.

Another way to overcome shyness is to act as if you're the host at your own party. If you act like the host, you'll be too busy making others feel comfortable to act shy. If you want to make others feel comfortable, look for someone who looks uncomfortable. You may be feeling every bit like they are, but if you see it as your responsibility to go over and make that person feel comfortable and drag him or her into a conversation, you'll forget that you were terribly uncomfortable yourself.

Don't expect to walk into a room of strangers and instantly mingle, crashing small clusters of people you don't know. That often works against you more than it promotes you. "Charismatic people aren't necessarily the life of the party," says Sally Quinn. "They look for people they know and talk to them. In more cases than not, their personalities are so engaging, that people who know them will immediately want to share them with others, and other people will want to get to know them."

Enthusiasm Counts—If You Show It Right

The conductor on the New York City subway train I catch each week-day morning has no patience for people who don't hustle. The subway train is the shuttle that runs between Times Square and Grand Central Terminal. After the train discharges passengers in Times Square, it sits there for a minute or two before leaving for the three-minute trip to the east side of Manhattan. When that train is ready to depart, you hear the motor switch on and the conductor say, "Watch the closing doors," and all the doors slide shut.

Recently, however, I began to notice that the train's new conductor was waiting a few extra seconds whenever people were jogging to make the train. I also noticed there were times when he'd close them up when passengers were walking toward the train. Curious about his motives, I asked what made him decide to hold the doors for some and close them on others. "If people are tryin', I'm buyin'," he said. "I like helping people who make an effort to get on. I'll hold the door a few extra seconds for them. But if catching this train doesn't matter to you, it sure doesn't matter to me. You can take the next one."

As I listened to that conductor, I realized that there are people like him all over, waiting to make a difference in your life if you show them you're willing to make an effort and that you're enthusiastic.

Jam is a prime example of someone who exudes enthusiasm and reaps the benefits. Anyone who has vacationed on the Caribbean island of St. Barts probably knows Jam. He runs a fabulous cigar shop in the village of St. Jean and can always be found making Cuban coffee or pouring out shots from a $500 bottle of thirty-year-old rum for regular customers who have stopped by. People fly their private jets in to St. Barts just to pick up cigars and shoot the breeze with Jam. I've even met people at parties in New York who know him.

What makes Jam so special is his intoxicatingly high level of enthusiasm and humility. No matter who is in his shop, he is upbeat, asking everyone how they're doing and giving them personal attention. As a result, he does a fabulous business. "I came from a poor background in Tunisia," he said. "I am excited to be living such a comfortable life now. I have a great wife and kids, and I love them very much. I love people. I enjoy their happiness and share mine with them. When I'm excited, they become more excited. They may come in serious or reserved because they don't know me, but they always leave in a better mood. I also love seeing how my personality rubs off on them. Sometimes my spirit makes them withdraw, but once they've been here a few times, they realize this is how I really am.

"Enthusiasm is catching. At first, you're afraid when someone is happy because you think the person is trying to get you to drop your guard so they can steal from you. But when you see that the enthusiastic person doesn't want anything, you become enthusiastic too. Enthusiasm is also good for business, but only because it makes doing business fun. Enthusiasm makes people excited and it makes them feel special. There are other places to buy cigars on this island—and all over the Caribbean. There are larger stores. But there is no other store where you're going to find me. Do people buy more cigars because of it? I don't know. I'm sure they do. But I do know that they're here for more than the cigars. They call months later to see how I'm doing, they send me gifts when they get home, they're just happy to have met me and I'm happy to have met them. Enthusiasm brings people to you—and people bring luck."

Showing enthusiasm isn't easy for some people, but it's essential for making luck. Showing your excitement is attractive because there's emotional virility attached to it. When you're excited, you are young and alive. When you make an effort to show your eagerness, your intentions and desires are clear, and more people want to make you happy. We like people who are excited about what they do, about life, about anything. It means they are alive and energetic, and helping them makes us feel energetic and alive.

Seek the Right Level of Enthusiasm

Not all people who are enthusiastic are turn-ons. Unlike Jam, there are plenty of people who come on too strong or whose enthusiasm isn't genuine. Their intense level of familiarity scares us, because we're afraid they're going to take advantage of us. For enthusiasm to be effective, it needs to be warm and inviting. Coming on strong singes the people you're trying to warm up.

I once knew this person who was so enthusiastic he made everyone with whom he came in contact feel uneasy. He was always dressed to kill, wore too much aftershave, stood too close to you, was hyperactive, and talked too fast. He certainly sounded optimistic and determined. He was always pumped up, always enthusiastic. His enthusiasm would attract attention, yet his high level of excitement rarely did him any good. No matter when I'd run into him, he'd be struggling professionally, and the more he'd struggle, the more enthusiastic he thought he had to become. Whenever I'd mention his name in passing to other people who knew him, they'd all have the same reaction: "He gives me the creeps."

For enthusiasm to be effective, it has to start out low-key. You can't use it like a baseball bat. There is a seductive quality about enthusiasm, and when it's used too aggressively or too intensively, the people you're trying to win over will wonder whether you have some hidden agenda, and they'll question your judgment. People aren't going to join you unless you coax them and show them you won't embarrass them. Your enthusiasm has to be infectious if it is to be effective, not paralyzing. People have to feel motivated by your spirit, not cornered or smothered by it. Too much enthusiasm makes you seem reckless and out of control, which won't help your cause.

Fast-talkers are enthusiastic, but their behavior makes us think they aren't worthy of what we have to offer. We associate people who walk and talk fast with people who are trying to cover up something or trying to distract us from the truth.

How Lucky People Show Enthusiasm— and Get Results

There are only two things we can control in life—our attitude and our effort. Enthusiasm is a direct reflection of both. Being enthusiastic conveys that you have a positive attitude and that you care. Enthusiasm makes people think there is an effervescent quality about you. Many lucky people know the importance of enthusiasm, but they also know that it comes in many different levels of intensity.

Here are lucky people's secrets about exuding enthusiasm . . .

• **Develop a "yearbook" smile.** One of the most effective ways to stick in people's minds is to smile broadly. Imagine you were handed a yearbook (not your own) and asked to look through it. And let's say that at the end you closed the yearbook and were asked to describe the most enthusiastic people in the book. I guarantee you'd recall the ones who were smiling broadest. Like the people in that yearbook, a big, genuine smile creates a lasting, enthusiastic image in the minds of the people you meet. A great smile helps you stand out because it says in the warmest way that you care about the person you've met. It also says that life treats you well, that life is easy, and that you're lucky, which is exactly the message you want to send out.

Every lucky person I know consciously smiles as often as possible. "Practicing your smile in a mirror is a stupid, five-second exercise," says a successful attorney I know. "But believe me, a smile can make a big difference in the amount of good fortune that comes your way. If you don't believe it, try it for a week and see."

In addition to making you more memorable, a smile has a few side benefits. Smiling helps you like yourself more, and it forces you to relax. It's very hard to remain angry or stressed out when you smile.

• **Customize your enthusiasm to fit the circumstances.** Different types of enthusiasm are required in different situations. A friend of mine who is exceptionally enthusiastic found that her fizzy spirit worked against her in a meeting when she started out in sales. She recalls that during this important data-presentation meeting, she turned on her enthusiasm to win over the people there. After the meeting, her boss took her aside and suggested she tone it down in the future. Her intense enthusiasm was making people think she was a lightweight.

Coming to terms with the downside of her high level of enthusiasm was extremely helpful in later years when my friend's upbeat personality was compromising an important business relationship. "I had this key contact who I felt was drifting away from me. We had a mutual friend, and when I mentioned the state of our relationship to her, she said the contact thought I was a bit of a phony. To give you an idea of the contrast, this contact's metabolism runs at zero. She's very low-key. Well I was blown away when I heard that, because this is who I really am. So I asked our mutual friend what she thought I should do to get the relationship back on track. She said that since she didn't think the person could boost her level of enthusiasm, it would probably be a lot easier if I toned mine down to a point where she and I could at least have professional admiration for each other.

"So instead of bounding into this person's office with, 'Hey, get this, this is great, you're going to love it!' I had to turn that into, 'Hi. You may find this interesting.' It was really tough for me to refine myself. But I found a way to do it. I taught myself to play defense. When meeting people, I always start out friendly but low-key. I turn up my enthusiasm depending on their response, being careful not to go too far and lose the person with whom I am trying to connect or win over."

• **Look deeply into their eyes.** Everyone I know who has met President Clinton says the same thing about him. When I asked them what makes him seem so special in person, they say it's his enthusiasm. "Love him or hate him, he makes you feel good by looking right at you and taking an interest in what you have to say," the wife of a fund-raising attorney told me. "Maybe he isn't listening, but he sure does a fantastic imitation of someone who is. My God, can you imagine? The president is taking an interest in you. But you know, I have to say, even if he wasn't the president, I would have been impressed. He looked at me in a way that made me feel he had come to see me, and on this day I was one of fifty people in the room. Everyone felt that way when we talked about it afterward."

As we discussed earlier, it's hard to look directly into people's eyes. Most people look away to gather their thoughts or express themselves. I have enormous trouble with this myself, and it's something I'm always trying to improve. At the same time, you don't want to look at someone so long that you make them uncomfortable or make it seem as if you don't understand what they're saying.

To make a connection just by using your eyes, imagine the other person's eyes are voice activators, and that you cannot talk unless you are looking at them. This seemingly silly exercise will at least get you in the habit of making eye contact. When the other person has finished talking, look at his or her eyes and count to three before speaking. This will enforce the impression that you're engrossed, you took it all in, and now you are responding thoughtfully and enthusiastically. Answering immediately or before someone is finished talking doesn't always mean you're enthusiastic. It can also mean you are rude or didn't hear a word that was said. The three-second delay is incredibly rewarding for the person who just finished speaking, and it will make them quickly warm up to you.

• **Be more enthusiastic about others than about yourself.** Even if you're not a naturally enthusiastic person, you can imitate the behavior of those who are. As most people know, when you ask someone lots of questions, you will almost always be viewed as incredibly interesting. The same is true for enthusiasm. The more pumped up you are about what the *other* person is telling you, the more you will be remembered as being enthusiastic.

Just make sure you have lots of questions, and remind yourself not to interrupt. Questions will make you seem eager and engaged. When you are eager and engaged, you will always be thought of as enthusiastic. Of course, you also need to be proud of yourself and ready to talk about your own accomplishments should the subject arise. But the more interested you are in others and the more confident you are in yourself, the more you will seem enthusiastic even if you're not at that moment.

Remember that charisma is the art of making people vividly aware that you are paying attention to them. Don't confuse charisma with egomania. Your efforts must be focused on feeding other people's desires to be noticed, not holding them captive as you talk about yourself. Constantly putting the spotlight on other people and praising their accomplishments leaves them feeling terrific about themselves and, by extension, you. The more your charisma touches the people around you, and the more special you make them feel, the more likely they'll be inspired to do anything for you.

CHAPTER EIGHT

LUCKY SECRET 3:
Become Known for Your Childlike Curiosity

The secret of genius is to carry the spirit of the child into old age.

ALDOUS HUXLEY

No matter how knowledgeable or experienced you think you are, you need something extra to make people want to go out of their way for you. For some lucky people, that something extra is an ability to be a little naïve.

Being a know-it-all may make you feel like a genius, but that attitude and approach to life almost always limits your opportunities. As impressive as intelligence and experience are, exhibiting a childlike innocence will make you seem vulnerable or slightly inferior to people who can help you. Being inferior is exactly where you want to be, because you won't be perceived as a threat. If people who hold opportunities feel superior to you, they will be more likely to help you. That's because when you're smart but just a little naïve, you become a worthy cause, and people will want to help you.

Innocence is not the same as ignorance. Innocence combines

119

honesty, purity, and respect for simplicity. Ignorance, on the other hand, is just plain dumb. What you want to project is a childlike curiosity. Children don't come to conclusions until they understand how things work. They keep an open mind and they aren't afraid to ask the questions most adults are too embarrassed to pose. Children don't pretend to have the answers to everything.

Age has a funny way of changing that. The more experienced we become, the harder it is to admit that we don't know something and the more likely we are to fake it. As we get older, we rush forward to demonstrate our knowledge. But this reflexive need to impress others with our intelligence has a big drawback: It limits the amount of information and help we could have received. If you have all the answers, you don't need help.

People like to help those who are just a little inferior but who are making an effort to improve themselves. Why? Because there's no threat and it's rewarding to help someone who is in need of advice and assistance.

What Is Childlike Curiosity?

Children are amazing. They always want to know how things work, and their search for the truth is relentless. They also force adults to find simple ways to explain the answers. My nine-year-old daughter recently wanted to know how money worked. Every time I tried to explain the concept of income, savings, and spending, it all sounded too complicated. She kept saying she didn't understand. Finally, I took her over to the kitchen sink. I turned on the water.

"See the water coming out? That's the money—and the reason why Mom and Dad go to work. Some people make a lot of water, and some people make a little. See the water backing up in the sink? That's good. We still have it. To save some of this good water, we put it in cups so we have some to pay the bills, buy food, eat out, go on vacation, buy you clothes, and other stuff. See the water going down the drain? That's spending. We try not to spend money on things we don't need, because we don't see the water again once it goes down the drain. We also try to make sure the water doesn't go down the drain faster than it's coming out of the faucet. Otherwise there's nothing for the cups. That's why we have to be careful with money."

My daughter was blown away and ran off yelling, "Hey Mom, do you know how money works? I do." Kids aren't ashamed to ask "Why?" But more important, they are unafraid to ask again and again until they are satisfied with the answers. They'll ask why until someone finally admits they don't know or takes the time to help them understand by speaking in simpler, easier-to-understand terms.

Asking "Why?" or saying "I don't understand" is hard for many adults. We're afraid people will think we're dumb. We also feel the need to impress people with our smarts or show them how clever we are.

But if you can rediscover and embrace your childlike curiosity, you won't be ashamed to say you don't know something or that you don't understand what you're being told. Adults with childlike curiosity become more animated with every answer they're given and are openly amazed by the explanations. Consciously keeping an open mind puts you in touch with your childlike side. Many successful people exhibit a childlike curiosity about things they're unfamiliar with that might benefit their business or creative endeavor.

Jim McCann, president of 1-800-FLOWERS, the world's largest florist, is one such curious person. "I'm not shy about asking people what they do and how they do it," says McCann. "That's the only way I can find out if there's some system or technique that's adaptable for my own business. Curiosity has a big benefit. When I ask dozens of dumb questions, I wind up with great answers and more information to help me make luck happen. I'm curious because I want to learn. Many of the big breakthroughs in business started out as a very simple idea that anyone else could have done. The difference between those who capitalize on a simple idea and those who don't is that those who do were just a little more curious than everyone else and didn't rest until their questions were answered."

You just need a bit of confidence and courage to let your curiosity show. Most people cover their knowledge gaps, thinking that to admit they don't know something will make them look ignorant and therefore not worthy of opportunity. In fact, asking simple questions means you're confident and self-assured.

"It's good to be a little dumber than everyone else so that you're not such a know-it-all," says Ben Bradlee, whose childlike curiosity as the former editor of the *Washington Post* helped expose the Watergate cover-up. "If you know a little bit about a lot of things and not a lot about much, life's a lot easier. People tell you things and help you. They feel a little sorry for you, in a good way.

"I had a very good education, but it wasn't long enough. I only made it through three years of college because of World War II. I never became an expert on a whole lot, and that turned out to be a big plus for me. A great journalist once told me that the essence of good journalism is superficiality. If you know everything about everything, you can't make up your mind about what is important."

Why Childlike Curiosity
Improves Your Luck

When you ask simple questions and avoid jumping to conclusions, you seem a little naïve. The more naïve you can seem, the more sophisticated you make others feel. This inquisitive behavior makes the other person feel safe and smart. And if they feel like a respected expert, they'll feel good about themselves and want to help you.

Whenever I'm in meetings and people ask "Why?" or "How does that work, I don't understand?" the first collective reaction is surprise. But the group's surprise almost immediately turns to relief as it becomes clear that others in the room had the same question but were too afraid to ask. Become someone who asks the simple questions and you become the most respected person in the room.

When you ask questions, you are showing your respect. But you are also doing something more subtle—you are demonstrating your interest and giving the other person a chance to explain. Everyone likes to explain what they know, especially when the question is simple. And here's the payoff: When the person is finished explaining the answer to you, instead of being viewed as a moron, which is what keeps most people from asking simple questions, you're viewed in a positive light. Keep in mind that nearly every brilliant invention, from the light bulb to the laptop computer, was invented because someone needed a simple solution to a complex problem, and the inventor needed to know how something worked.

Asking simple questions makes luck happen. "By asking questions and keeping an open mind, more things will come to you," says Ben Bradlee. "Believe it or not, I'm not very political. I simply want to know what is happening rather than whether something is right or wrong. Then I take a lot of time to make up my mind about them. With Watergate, we were lucky at the *Post* that Nixon thought we were fools. Of course, we weren't. But he thought he could steamroller us, and he couldn't. We were lucky in our enemies back then. They underestimated the intelligence of the people searching for the truth, the people asking the dumb questions."

How to Develop a Childlike Curiosity

A childlike curiosity is nothing more than being fascinated by what's being said and showing it. Instead of trying to show how smart you are, it's far more productive and beneficial to find out how smart others are.

Here are the strategies of people with a childlike curiosity . . .

• **Let kids be your role model.** Bobby McFerrin, the vocalist, musical innovator, and ten-time Grammy Award–winner who is widely known for writing and recording the 1988 pop hit *Don't Worry, Be Happy,* is completely in touch with his childlike curiosity. It helps him to embrace the learning process rather than be intimidated by it. Shortly after *Don't Worry, Be Happy,* he took a big risk by taking a sabbatical from pop music and focused on studying to be an orchestra conductor and writing an opera.

"My decision was largely influenced by my curiosity and interest in continually learning and challenging myself," McFerrin says. His initial curiosity about conducting led him to Leonard Bernstein, whom he first met while performing at Bernstein's seventieth birthday celebration at the Tanglewood Music Festival in 1988. He was taken by Bernstein's musicianship, brilliance, and charisma. So McFerrin wrote him a simple letter after the concert asking if he could have a conducting lesson. Bernstein invited him up to Tanglewood the next summer. That year McFerrin spent three weeks at the music center in Massachusetts, attending master conducting classes and taking a private lesson with Bernstein.

But the complex orchestral scores were intimidating, even though McFerrin reads music and had grown up in a family of musicians. "When I saw the score, I said to Bernstein, 'So many different instruments playing so many different notes.' Bernstein understood exactly what I meant, and he felt my apprehension. He knew that I had spent most of my career as a jazz singer and musician. So he simplified the whole process of conducting for me by saying, 'Bobby, it's just jazz. It's just lots of instruments playing music.'"

Such an honest, down-to-earth response from someone like Bernstein helped McFerrin relax and absorb Bernstein's wisdom. Bernstein's words also gave McFerrin the confidence to approach conducting and classical music on his terms. "Had I spent the entire time with Bernstein trying to impress him, I probably wouldn't have learned much that summer."

Motivated by his work with Bernstein in 1989, McFerrin went on to be a guest conductor with most of the world's great orchestras. In 1995, he moved his wife and three children to Minneapolis, where he was offered the position of "creative conductor" with the St. Paul Chamber Orchestra. Instead of suppressing his playful side in the classical world, McFerrin adapted it to his performances, and audiences of adults and children have responded with tremendous support.

"I believe in positive simplicity," McFerrin says. "If you remain true to the child inside of you and listen to your heart, you will excel at whatever you do. Watch kids carefully, and try to understand why they do what they do. Children are a never-ending source of amazement and insight for me. They can teach you a lot about yourself and what's truly important in life."

• **Ask enough questions of key people until they become interested in you.** Jim McCann's big break came in 1989 at a direct marketing conference in Atlanta where he went to hear Ted Turner speak. At the time, McCann had flower-shop affiliates around the country delivering nationwide to customers who called 1-800-FLOWERS. But he needed help getting his company's message out.

"After the seminar, I cornered Turner and asked him dozens of basic questions about CNN and his business. I guess somewhere along the line he became tired of answering them and became more interested in knowing what I did. When I told him, he immediately became pumped up about my company. I'll never forget his words. He said, 'Son, we're going to hook you up and see if we can help you take your business to another level.' At the time, CNN needed a poster child for its station because it wasn't sold out of advertising.

"Shortly after our meeting, I entered into a favorable advertising schedule with CNN that greatly increased my company's profile. I learned two important lessons that day: If you sound help-able rather than helpless, opportunity will rush to you. Also, if you're curious rather than cocky, people will eventually get around to asking what kind of help you need rather than trying to get away from you. Had I aggressively tried to sell Ted Turner on my company right off the bat, he would have blown me off."

So how do you ask questions in a way that they sound smart and not stupid? Jim McCann says he starts out by saying, "I must confess, I don't know your world all that well, but one question I have is . . ." That disarms people and gets them to think about how they can help you. You become a worthy cause not because you seem pathetic but because you seem deserving of a break.

• **Resist the temptation to answer your own questions.** To develop a childlike curiosity, you have to do much more than ask lots of questions. Questions are merely a way to begin relationships. Your curiosity must grow as your questions are answered. Unlucky people don't listen to answers. They ask questions but immediately begin thinking of their next question. Or they try to come up with a clever answer to finish the other person's sentence. But you'll never be considered someone worth helping if the impression people have of you is that you're a scheming questioner rather than a patient listener.

Patient listeners know that the really good information doesn't come until a minute or two into an answer. If you cut off the person talking, you could miss out on a great piece of information. Patient listeners wait until answers are nearly complete before asking another question. They may even wait until the person is done and pause for a moment to show that they are listening and savoring what's being said. This reaction often encourages the person talking to go further and share more information.

A great way to assess your ability to listen is to ask if you can tape one of your phone conversations with a friend. As an editor and writer, I often record the people I'm interviewing so that I can accurately capture their points and tone when I write. When I first started out, I was often annoyed by the foolishness of my impatience. I would hear the person on the tape getting warmed up to tell me something important, only to hear myself interrupt him or her with a question. Invariably, we never returned to the point that was about to be developed.

"My father used to tell me every now and then, the wisdom of the ages cries out for silence," Ben Bradlee says. "I've said that a hundred times if I've said it once. It really isn't crucial to have an immediate response to everything you hear or that you reach judgments automatically or immediately. I know some people who, no matter what you say, have a quick answer and a quick opinion. Sometimes you get more when you don't voice an opinion."

▪CHAPTER NINE▪

LUCKY SECRET 4:
Simplify Other People's Lives

If you want to lift yourself up, lift up someone else.
BOOKER T. WASHINGTON

When you make sacrifices for people without expecting or asking for repayment, you double your chances of receiving good fortune. For one, the joy created by your generosity will make you feel good about yourself. When you feel good about yourself, you feel more optimistic, which automatically makes you someone other people will want to help. For another, the people you've helped will go out of their way to help you—even if you weren't expecting help when you lent support. Generosity is contagious.

But freely letting go of the things we cherish—whether it's time, energy, resources, or contacts—without an up-front guarantee of repayment is hard. The things we value are hard to come by and even harder to replace. We're also reluctant to give because we're concerned that our gift won't be appreciated or that it won't be used the way we wish. Or it will be destroyed or abused. Or we may never again hear from the person we've helped. So most people extend themselves only when they're sure the exchange rate will be equitable. But that's not quite generosity. When your gift has strings attached, you only get back the value of what you gave up. Truly generous people get back much more, because true generosity is selfless and stirs others to be generous in return.

Generosity's payoff is tremendous. Of the many lucky people I know, all are truly generous with their time, money, or resources. They are very giving people. They are always happy to improve people's lives if they can. But their assistance isn't purely random. They are highly selective about who benefits from their generosity. When they give, they aren't expecting much more than thanks in return. What motivates them to be generous is first and foremost a deep sense of charity and a desire to give back a little of the good fortune they have experienced. When you learn to share unconditionally, your chances of success soar.

Why Generosity Makes You Look Lucky

By nature, we stockpile those things that ensure our survival and support our success. Hoarding and even greed have anthropological roots, dating back thousands of years to a time when food was scarce and provisions had to be hidden away. Despite fatter times, we still hold on to what we've earned and what is precious because we're never sure when we'll need it or whether we will have enough of it.

We resist giving up what we prize because we don't perceive there's much value in generosity. It's not our fault. We live in a society where everything has a specific value and exchange rate. We work, we expect to get paid. We want something at the store, the store expects us to pay for it. We help people out of a tough spot, and we count the days waiting for our favor to be returned. When we pick up the tab at a restaurant, we immediately agree that the other person will pay the next time. It's a tit-for-tat world, and nearly everything we give or get comes with a price or conditions. Even if that price isn't immediately disclosed, it's always implied.

We also resist giving up the things we hold dear because we aren't confident that they will be appreciated or cared for properly. Most people give only when they feel that the person receiving their gift will benefit and won't make them look bad. For example, we are less likely to pass along someone to an important contact if that person is rude or inept. Our reputation and judgment are at stake, and we instinctively won't risk that for someone who isn't likely to benefit or profit from the experience or who will inadvertently hurt us in the process.

To understand the spirit of generosity, you have to shift your focus from how giving will help you to how your assistance will benefit the person you're helping. You can be as selective as you wish with your help, so long as your motive is to help someone else rather than yourself. Dr. Bernie Siegel, one of the country's leading experts on the connection between a positive mind and a healthy body, believes that to be truly giving requires a passion for making others' lives easier.

"A few years ago I was gifted a great deal of money, which I passed along to our five children," he says. "A short time later one of our sons asked if he could borrow some money. When I asked what happened to the money I gave him, he told me he gave his share to a young man from another country, so that the man could go to college. At the time, I hit the roof. Our son's generosity was costing me money. A short time later I realized what a wonderful thing my son had done. I apologized and told him it wasn't up to me to tell him what to do with my gift. I learned a valuable lesson there. When you try to determine what people should do with what you've given them, it's no longer a gift."

While giving up what we love without expectation of repayment is hard, generosity is nearly always appreciated more than we realize. If you make someone's life easier without implying that there's a price tag on your effort, your sacrifice won't be forgotten. Generosity breeds loyalty. You experience this every time a store or restaurant manager does something for you. As a result, you're likely to patronize that store or restaurant over and over again. Similarly, if someone does a good deed for you, you feel grateful and are likely to help the person even more than they helped you.

I tend to be a very giving person, with both praise and opportunity. I don't expect my praise or favors to be returned. It's just part of my mission to help people the way I've been helped in my career. Yet, somehow, opportunities have always come back to me when I've least expected them.

"Generous people attract other generous people," says Dr. Siegel. "They inspire each other. Greedy, angry people wear you out if you stay with them too long. For instance, I often give help to struggling artists I've read about in the local paper. I like artists because they are trying to improve their lives by bringing joy to other people's lives. If I can make an artist's life a little easier, that person becomes a friend of mine. I expect nothing in return. Just knowing a person like that makes me feel great. They enrich my life."

But being generous makes you look lucky. There's nothing you can do about that. Giving up the things you love sends a very positive signal. If you can part easily with things that you revere, people assume that you must be able to replace those things easily and without much effort. The other reason why giving makes us seem lucky is the spiritual dimension we assume. The positive aspects of charity and helping the less fortunate are acknowledged in almost every religion and culture, and are always equated with goodness and even holiness.

"I learned about the spirit of giving from my father," Siegel says. "My father's father died when my father was quite young. His mother was left with six children, and my father said he had to learn how to earn money and appreciate what it was useful for. Among its best uses, he said, was to help other people. I remember when I was struggling through medical school, I wanted to get married and didn't have enough money. I was twenty-one years old at the time, and I felt very guilty when I had to ask my father for money. He could see how difficult it was for me to ask considering he was already helping me with tuition costs. I'll never forget what he said when he gave me the money. He said, 'I can say no to you, but I believe that this is what money is for. Making someone's life easier.' When you grow up with a father who says this, you have a very different outlook on money."

James O'Shaughnessy, one of the country's most successful and driven money managers I know, takes great pleasure in being generous and patient with everyone he meets. "I know how lucky I am and how fortunate I've been. When I help someone, I expect nothing in return. If I can give back some of the luck I've made, I'll be even. I even have dreams in which my generous nature is challenged. In one I've had repeatedly recently, my wife and I are sitting on the back of this magnificent boat, and there's a woman sitting there who's a guest of ours.

"In a glass case is a beautiful vase that this woman can't stop looking at. She goes on and on about how much she admires the vase. She says, 'It's the most beautiful vase in the world. I've never seen a vase this beautiful.' So I turn to her and say, 'It's yours.' And she says, 'I could never, ever, ever accept this gift because it is way too costly.' And I say, 'No really, you must take it. It's yours.' She says, 'No really, I can't.' So I tell her that unless she takes it, I'll throw it into the sea. The dream usually ends with me telling her that things in and of themselves have no value to me. I don't know what this dream means, but that's how I live my life."

Give Without Expecting Anything in Return

Perhaps the biggest mistake people make when they give is that they expect to be repaid and fast. They also expect the returned favor to be of equal value or greater than what they originally gave up. In reality, most gifts and favors aren't returned immediately. Sometimes it's years before the person you helped turns around and helps you. Or the person you helped may never be able to help you or may not have anything to offer. If the favor is returned quickly, the odds are it won't meet your expectations. When you expect repayment, you are setting yourself up for disappointment and you're limiting your luck. You sour your attitude and outlook, and become bitter and resentful. When the person can't deliver what you had hoped, your resentment can turn to hostility, anger, and even greed. These negative emotions tarnish your lucky outlook and your lucky image.

That's why giving must be motivated by the true spirit of generosity. You have to give and then forget about it. Otherwise you are treating your gift as an investment, and when you do that, you can go crazy waiting for it to pay off.

You also can't give to everyone you meet or you'll have nothing left for yourself. You don't want to become a soft touch—someone on whom people become dependent for constant favors. These people can drain you. "Hey, there's generosity and then there's stupidity," says Siegel. "If I'm in a business deal and I have a contract with someone, I may sue if I don't get satisfaction. Generosity depends on the spirit and intentions of everyone involved. Giving is great, but only if your gift is put to positive use. I'm not going to help a drug addict destroy himself, for instance.

"Provided that I know my sacrifice isn't for anything harmful, I'm happy to give. If I ask what someone is going to do with my gift, it's merely because I want that person to know that I care about him or her. But if the person can't respond to my question, and isn't ready to take care of himself and love himself, I won't get involved in perpetuating their self-destruction."

To be truly generous, don't spend too much time thinking about what you've done for others, only about what others are doing with the gifts you've given them.

Give to the Appreciative, and Opportunity Will Follow

Sir John Marks Templeton, the great financier and philanthropist, once told me something I've never forgotten. He said that generosity's true reward is the warmth you feel after you've given to a worthy cause. The recipient of your gift feels joy, but the pleasure you experience giving should be just as intense. When you give to someone who appreciates your gift, you've enriched your spirit, and nothing else really matters.

Lucky people give in ways that help people. In return their images and reputations are enhanced. The many lucky people I know give unconditionally, but most of the people they help want more than anything to return the favors. The more they give, the luckier they become because their efforts are selfless and without condition, which causes people to want to repay them.

Acts of generosity cause people to admire the fact that you went out on a limb for them. In return, they will work hard to repay you. You may not even be aware they're helping you. The returned favor may be to recommend you for a big opportunity. Generosity guarantees you a place at the top of people's lists, which is often all you need to greatly improve your luck.

Here's how lucky people extend their generosity . . .

• **Give when your generosity will build high-quality friendships.**
While you can't give to everyone you meet—nor should you—one of
the best reasons to give is to make a friend. Lucky people assist people
they'd like to know better. A rather well-known and wealthy stock
market investor told me over lunch that it has always been his policy
to make as many opportunities as possible available to the people he
considers friends. When you trust the judgment and integrity of
someone, he said, help that person any way you can.

"That person will always be on an upward, positive track, and will
always be there for you," he advised. "When I got out of college just
after World War II, I got a decent job at a major brokerage and spent
my first year getting everyone I knew a job. I did everything I could to
help them get their feet in the doors of brokerages and accounting
firms in New York. I guess I was sort of their agent. My motive wasn't
to collect a fee. I really liked these guys. I had gone to Princeton with
them. These jobs weren't major positions, but they were a start.

"Nearly every one of these guys has become a household name.
On their way up over the years, they never forgot my generosity. Their
help has been invaluable to me. I never asked for repayment, but I was
repaid on a scale that far exceeded what I had done for them. It's
astonishing. Big favors for people you consider friends pay off in a
huge way, despite the fact that you may not want anything in return.
Funny thing is that ever since I helped them, my friends have always
thought of me as lucky, even though I think I had to work a lot harder
than they did to get where I am today."

• **Give when people are down on their luck.** One of the best
times to offer assistance is when people are facing hard times. That's
when most people desert them and that's when these people need the
most support. They also won't ever forget your help. The goal here

isn't to profit from their misery but to help the people you value get back on their feet. When you rush in to help someone whom few others will even talk to, you look lucky because you're tempting fate. You're like the doctor treating someone with a contagious illness. Helping people when they're down takes a great deal of courage, and that fortitude makes you seem lucky, since only someone who is magically protected from the same fate would dare risk making that person a cause.

I know the owner of a company in Texas who is tremendously skillful at helping friends who are in a bad way. He's the first to help people who have been laid off or are struggling. Sometimes it's through a pep talk, or he'll offer them consulting work. "The easy thing to do is to ignore these people," he says. "Who wants to get close to people who are having bad luck or might be perceived as losers? You have to be crazy. But that's when a little help goes a long way. I can't realistically give these people millions of dollars or get their jobs back for them. But I can give them comfort at a time of great uncertainty and fear. If I can provide these people with a little temporary shelter from their storm, it's just enough for them to regain their balance.

"Once they're strong enough to move on, they never forget what I've done. Mind you, I don't do it to be repaid. Many people I've helped this way have never given me anything back, and I hope they never do. But over the years, many have sent me great job candidates, tipped me off to wonderful business opportunities, and given me fantastic advice. People never forget your help when they're down. They're grateful because they really needed it. But they also know they might not have had the courage to do what you did had you been in the same situation. It takes enormous strength to help someone who is down. But once they're on their feet, you've made a business partner for life. You'll be flooded with opportunities."

• **Giving is important, but so is following up with additional help.** Helping friends or business colleagues when they need it most will make you look lucky. But following up and providing additional support makes it clear that you really care. Anyone who is hard-working and honorable won't ask you for additional assistance after you've provided it initially. That's why a follow-up call to them is so greatly appreciated. Most people do not bother to take this step. They give and forget, hoping never to hear from the person again.

When you follow up to be sure that your initial generosity was beneficial, you're standing by the quality of your assistance. Like a good carpenter who calls to make sure you love your bookshelves, you are checking up on the happiness of your customer. That extra effort also makes your help more memorable because it shows you truly care.

I know a senior executive at a well-known apparel company in the Midwest who is famous for her follow-up. "Friends are so amazed when I call to find out if my aid was helpful," she says. "They just assume that they had only one rub of the lamp and that if nothing resulted from my help, they'd have to turn to another friend. I usually call about a month after I've given them a lead to see what happened. For the first few minutes of my call, they usually try to put their best face forward. 'Oh yeah, everything is great. I have high hopes,' they say.

"But I want the truth. What good is my help if it wasn't helpful? If I feel that my initial efforts weren't worthwhile, I'll line up others until it works out for them. Sure, sometimes it's the other person's fault and they're blowing opportunities. But they're not blowing those opportunities on purpose. I usually keep at them until they beg me to stop calling. When you make the extra effort and surprise people, they're so grateful. They see you as some kind of savior. Most people hesitate to mention that your help might not have been that effective.

They're afraid you'll feel that they let you down if your generosity didn't produce results. But if you beat them to it, you'll always be in their hearts."

• **Give something else if you can't give what was requested.** Sometimes we're asked for things we just can't provide. I'm often cold-called by freelance writers who want assignments. But if they don't specialize in a subject that I need covered, I can't give them work. However, if I respect them I'll always refer them to another editor at another magazine. I'll even call the other editor to let them know the writer will be calling. Most people just need hope to help them get to the level they're trying to reach. Providing them with hope doesn't cost anything and is also highly appreciated.

Jim McCann, president of 1-800-FLOWERS, has an interesting philosophy. "I approach life with the idea that I own this very unusual bank account. Unlike any other bank account, the more I give away, the greater the balance in the account. My gifts don't have to be large. They can be as little as an acknowledgment, a pat on the back, or a compliment about how someone has handled a job. The more I give out, the bigger the balance. Whether it's someone I come across who is changing careers or looking for an opportunity, I keep that person's dream on my list. Then I try to find something I can refer to them.

"Will my effort have a payback? Who cares. What I have found in the course of my good life is that whether or not favors come back to me, that type of generosity will serve me well over and over again."

■ CHAPTER TEN ■

LUCKY SECRET 5:
Let Powerful People Own a Piece of You

Those who deserve recognition for their efforts
should be honoured accordingly.

THE BIBLE

One of the hardest things to share is credit for a great idea. We tend to become angry and resentful when even partial ownership is claimed for the concepts we consider our own. It's difficult to admit that someone else influenced our thinking. It's also human nature to want full recognition for our originality and accomplishments.

Why are we so proprietary about the creative process? When all is said and done, we are the sum total of our ideas and creativity. That's why we hate it when people try to share authorship of our ideas. We feel violated, as if someone stole from us. We are angry that the attention we worked so hard to attract must be diluted. It's not that we are paranoid. We just know how easy it is for people to convince themselves that our brainstorms are also theirs.

A good idea is easy to steal. All people have to do is have an opinion about your idea, and in a flash they believe they are the idea's creator. If you subsequently refuse to share credit, these people will convince themselves that you stole the idea from them. Why? For one, they might be right. He or she may have had more of an impact on your original idea than you are willing to admit. For another, even though the person's input may have been nothing more than a suggestion, it's human nature to want to be thought of as a creative thinker.

While it rarely makes sense to give total credit for your great ideas, denying other people even partial credit can be just as foolish. Denying people credit limits your luck because it shuts people out—people who can help you. Shut people out and you've made enemies, and enemies can limit the amount of opportunities that come your way. When you give credit where credit is due, you give up a small piece of your ego and you make yourself instantly more likable. To look lucky, however, you have to be selective about who gets credit and how you recognize their contributions.

Let Others Own a Piece of You

Recognize the people who helped you come up with your big ideas and they will become partners in your enterprise. Acknowledge the people who contributed to your ideas and they automatically will have an interest in seeing you succeed. They also will make opportunities available to you because now they are part of the endeavor. Their own egos are on the line. Your success is their success, and if you give them credit for participating, they will want to help you succeed again and again. Your project suddenly becomes their responsibility as well as yours.

If someone played a role in helping you shape an idea, that effort, no matter how small, should be recognized. Recognition has a powerful, long-term payoff. When you give someone credit, they will champion your thoughts as if they were their own and they will steer more opportunities your way.

Giving credit requires not only generosity but courage and honesty, and when you give it, you'll be admired. "People who give credit to other people usually wind up in the center and become the primary movers and shakers of any team," says Stephen Covey, the great expert on leadership and human behavior. "They don't really care about keeping all of the credit. They care about the project, the idea, the goal, and that makes them worthy of help. That sense of selflessness is very powerful. Recognize other people, and they will feel valued by you. Humility draws people to you. Your strengths will seem to exceed other people's strengths.

"That kind of *abundance mentality* is common among people who generate luck. The whole concept of becoming vulnerable and ego-less is possible for people who share credit because deep down, they are anchored. Their sense of self is protected. It's safeguarded through an integrity source, which is why they can afford to give other people credit without having ego hangups."

The integrity source Covey refers to is positive values, which in turn make us comfortable with ourselves. When we're in touch with this inner source of strength, we are secure and self-satisfied enough to give others credit for their input.

Sharing in the rewards for a job well done—even when those rewards are nonmonetary—makes people feel positive about themselves. When you invite colleagues or coworkers into your limelight, you become an energy source and others will want to keep you at center stage. The outcome will be gifts in the form of expanded opportunities.

The Rewards of Sharing the Spotlight

Before you can learn the secret ways in which lucky people give credit and win opportunities, you must first overcome your natural resistance to sharing the spotlight. To get what you want you have to get over your emotional attachment to your ideas.

Here's how to avoid the mental traps that keep us from
acknowledging other people's input . . .

• **Don't assume everyone is trying to steal your ideas.** Think
about it. The big reason we hesitate to give credit for a brainstorm is
the fear that other people will be thought of as the brains behind what
we created. We all want to believe that we're brilliant and have original
ideas. When our intelligence is recognized, we instinctively crave
every ounce of that attention. Why? Perhaps because we fear that if
others are recognized, we will doubt the potency of our own creative
abilities, or it will confirm that we're impostors. Or perhaps we'll
believe we aren't as smart as we thought. There's also a part of us that
wants to do everything by ourselves and reap the full reward by solving
the problem single-handedly.

Unfortunately, all of these thoughts are counterproductive to making
good luck happen. The reality is that a great idea will stand for itself,
no matter who shares credit for it. The idea will still be considered
yours, even if you recognize the help you've had.

I once knew someone who felt so strongly about a computer
database she created that she would never let anyone feel as if they had
helped her create it. She also would never take suggestions for improving
or changing it. Whenever someone had an idea, she would ignore it and
defensively complain that people were trying to climb on the bandwagon after she had done all of the work. She was way too close to her
creation. Everyone knew the database was her idea. But once her
genius was initially recognized, she should have acknowledged others.

Then a strange thing happened. The more proprietary and pro-
tective she became about the database, the more she saw her colleagues as her enemies. She became defensive whenever anyone
made a suggestion to improve the database and angry when her own
suggestions to alter it were rejected. A tug of war began and, in the

end, management of the database was taken away from her and the people she tried to freeze out took over.

• **Think of your ideas as the swings in a public playground.** Another reason we hate to share credit for an idea is that we think of our brainstorms as private property and other people as trespassers. If you think of your ideas as *public* property instead, you won't be so defensive. Imagine you are the architect of public playgrounds. Now imagine your ideas are the swings, seesaws, and sandboxes. Instead of having the urge to shut people out, you will feel a desire to encourage them to play on what you've built. You want people to have fun in your park, to use the stuff. The happier they are, the more likely they are to invite other people, who will have opportunities for you.

Of course, you don't want them to take over your playground and throw you out. Telling someone thanks for helping you come up with a great idea or singling people out for their assistance must be done delicately and skillfully, always leaving you in the middle, not on the sidelines. But locking everyone out never helps you get what you want. Think of your ideas as playthings, and people will feel great after they've played with them. And that's exactly where you want them. Happy and grateful.

• **Long-term respect beats a few seconds of fame.** The reason we're reluctant to give credit to others is that we want to grab all of the attention ourselves. But that attention often lasts about thirty seconds—or however long it takes for someone to pat you on the back. If you insist on being a self-sufficient hero, you will cause people to fear you and even to work against you.

On the other hand, it pays to be known as someone who needs help and rewards assistance. When you offer people a chance to participate and then give them credit for their efforts, they respect and admire you—and your rewards will be much greater in the long run.

So figure out a way to demonstrate that others can benefit from helping you, and you will benefit as well.

If you can cause people to talk about you in the most glowing terms when you're not around, whatever part of your ego you had to give up will be well worth the sacrifice. There is nothing more important than your good name, and nothing improves your standing faster than allowing people to join in your celebration or become part of your success.

Of course, you'll have to be on guard for people who take advantage of your willingness to share the attention. But letting colleagues who deserve it feel part ownership in your idea is a worthwhile investment because they'll spread the good word about you. And reputation rules when it comes to luck.

• **Ideas are nothing more than incomplete projects.** Too many people put way too much emphasis on ideas. I have been in meetings where people fight like dogs for their ideas and become insulted when their ideas are challenged. It's easy to see why. Behind every idea is time spent thinking about it, and the very integrity of how we think is on the line. What we often lose sight of, however, is that ideas are just intentions and visions. You'll create more good luck if you think of your ideas as nothing more than ways to motivate people to help you get what you want. Remember, ideas are like dreams: They cannot be realized unless you have help.

• **Praise others as often as possible.** When you warmly praise people's efforts, you are expressing your gratitude and appreciation. We all want to be told we've done a good job, yet so many of us neglect to mention it to others. We hold back our praise because we believe that the recognition will spoil them—or that praising them will diminish our own endeavors.

If you can get over both hangups and regularly tell people that you appreciate what they've done for you, you will have made friends for life. If you ignore your colleagues' or coworkers' or assistants' efforts, some of them will go out of their way to make sure your life is more difficult than it has to be.

For example, I know two people who park their cars in New York City garages. The rate is expensive—around $350 a month. One of these guys is on a first-name basis with the attendants, taking a few minutes each day to ask their advice about cars or talk to them about sports. By talking to the attendants, he has shown that he respects them. This guy's car is always parked in the front of the garage, and he doesn't have a mark on it.

The other guy arrogantly comes and goes, never bothering to even look at the attendants, let alone make friendly conversation. They park his car in the back, and he has nicks and scratches on the doors from being parked too close to other cars.

The point here is that acknowledging the efforts and accomplishments of people with whom you come in contact will get them to look out for you and even help you if they can. You want people to rush forward and help you as soon as they see you coming.

Ask Key People for Advice . . . and Then Give Them Credit

Seek the advice of key people and let them share the credit for your achievements, and they will help you make good luck happen. But how you seek the advice of influential people and how you thank them will make a big difference in the quality of luck you will receive. Be smart enough to keep them abreast of your activities, and you will get what you want, fast.

Here's how the lucky people I know use this strategy effectively . . .

• **Target the people who can help you the most.** The people I know who are great at setting aside their egos and giving credit in ways that improve their luck have a great eye for people with resources. They always manage to acknowledge people who have lots of contacts and who can help them. It would be unfair to call these lucky people "users" because they aren't selfish or greedy people. Users take and take until there's nothing left. Then they move on, discarding the people who are no longer of use to them. Lucky people are smart, polite, and gracious. They pinpoint people who can help them, seek their advice, and give them credit for their accomplishments.

Where do you find key people who will find you attractive enough to help? A lucky senior advertising executive I know at one of the major movie studios told me he started by looking for powerful people at his company who needed help in areas of advertising with which they weren't fully familiar. "After I had been at the studio for about seven years, I still couldn't break through to the next level. The people I reported to saw me doing the job I held forever. Then a new top executive was added to the department. I decided to become that person's guide, showing him the ropes, helping him navigate, explaining the players and the dynamics. I was doing it for the good of the company and out of my own self-interest.

"As he moved up, he took ownership of me and gave me exposure to high-level people here who suddenly saw me in a different light. I would give him dozens of ideas and make him believe they were his. The whole game of success at any company is getting exposure to people at higher and higher levels. I let this executive in on the secrets of my job and gave him credit all the time. Because I was honest and extremely loyal, it was in his best interest to keep me close, and that's a beautiful place to be. Who cares if people thought the ideas were his. I looked at those ideas as my admission price to greater exposure. My job was to help that person shine, and in return he allowed me to shine."

But don't you risk giving away so many secrets of your job that the key person can replace you? "The secret is not to let the person in on the most important details of what you're telling him. You want to keep the other person informed in the broadest sense, but not about how you do it. Make the key person think the idea is his or hers, but don't provide too many details about how you do your job. You want the person to think he can't live without you."

Always associate with people who are smart and work hard. These people will always pass you on to other smart, hard-working people. These are the ones who can really improve your luck.

• **Know when to put yourself second.** People with access to opportunity are more likely to help you if they feel they have a stake in your achievement. I have found that there's nothing more powerful than asking people what they think and quietly listening to their responses. When you put yourself second, you are putting them first and acknowledging the importance and brilliance of their ideas.

A friend who has moved up quickly while working for a major children's Web site says she always puts herself second when she's with her boss. "It's amazing how successful you can be if you can visualize yourself as Robin instead of Batman," she says. "By always remembering your second-place position, you will make the people who can help you want you to do well. You will also keep them from thinking you've betrayed them. A top executive who had been my boss's rival left here recently. Shortly afterward, she called me for lunch. Now, it's in my best interest to have lunch with this person because who knows where she's going to end up. She could be of tremendous help to me. But if I have lunch with her and my boss finds out, I'm dead.

"So I told my boss that this person called and asked me to have lunch. I told her that there probably would be a few dishy stories about other executives at lunch. Then I asked my boss whether she thought I should go. Of course, my boss said yes, seeing only what was of interest to her—the gossip. My boss didn't see it as a career lunch. I'm just going to get the dirt and share my lunchtime stories with her. You always want to be truthful, but it's important to position things in a way that won't hurt the feelings of the person who is number one."

• **Show key people how their help made a difference.** One of the shrewdest ways to get people to help you is to show them how their advice changed you, your work, or your good fortune. It's one thing to ask people for their advice. It's another to show them how that advice had an impact on you. Such a move is confirmation that you take their advice and wisdom seriously. It also encourages them to help you get to the next level.

An artist friend of mine recently had one of her sculptures acquired by one of New York's most prestigious fine art museums. Artists are notoriously jealous people, since what makes one artist's work sell for tens of thousands of dollars and another's languish on the wall is often impossible to figure out. But this sculptor worked hard to overcome the randomness of those odds. Not only is she a superb artist, she also studies what successful artists do to become visible and get their works to sell.

"Look, I realized long ago that there are only a handful of genius artists whose works are so powerful and amazing that the works sell themselves," she says. "At the next level down, there are hundreds of artists whose works are very good, but not all of these artists make it. There isn't enough room in the museums and galleries, nor is there that much commercial demand for all of them. The difference, therefore, rests not in the art itself but in how well you are able to get others to promote you."

My friend is an excellent artist, but to break out of the pack, she had to rely on her other strengths—her openness and generosity of spirit. Some years ago, she met a curator from the prestigious museum at a show exhibiting the works of several artists. He made some critical suggestions about how she might change the direction of her work. Rather than succumb to her emotional instinct to dismiss the curator as a museum bureaucrat who had no business telling her how to create her art, she remained open-minded and took his advice.

When she had her own show recently, she sent him an invitation and wrote him a note telling him how much help his advice had been and that he should come see for himself. When he came to her show, she pointed out how his earlier critique had influenced her contemporary work. Later that week, he called her to say that he had recommended that the museum acquire one of her works. By giving up a small percentage of her ego and allowing the curator to become a part of her work, my friend was able to make good luck happen in a way that most artists just dream about.

"You have to be generous in this world," she says. "The curator's original comments were good, and I wanted him to see that. Seeing his influence in my work made him feel special and, in turn, he fought for me, as if my work were partly his."

• **Provide luck-makers with regular updates.** Asking someone for input or advice and then not giving him or her an update on how you're doing is a big mistake. When you ask for help, you have effectively sold a piece of yourself. You owe your "investors" regular reports. Providing updates of your progress keeps key people motivated to continue sending opportunities your way—especially if the one they gave you fails to deliver.

A friend of mine who holds a big job at a major software company in California illustrated this point with a story: "Last summer, an intern who worked for me said he wanted to go to law school. Just after he left the job to study for the entrance exams, he sent me an e-mail asking if I would write him a letter of recommendation to the law school he wanted to attend. So I wrote him a great letter. About three months later, I got another e-mail from him telling me that the school accepted him and that he was sure my letter had a great deal to do with his admittance. Whether or not that was true, I felt great. Then recently he e-mailed me again, asking if he could work as a temp for the upcoming summer. We had already filled the position, but I created a temp job for him. Isn't it funny how something as silly as courtesy e-mails can make or break your luck?"

• **Don't get greedy.** A big mistake many people make when friends or contacts provide them with help is expecting a miracle. They count on their key contacts to give them whatever they want whenever they need it. The problem is that people put too much faith in too few key contacts. They expect these influential people to make their lives easier on demand.

What impatient people fail to remember is that key contacts are busy. Sometimes they can't help you in the way you'd like. But that's no reason to write them off. What you never want to do is make your key people feel guilty about not being able to help you. Even if they can't give you the break you need, or they pass you along to people who aren't very helpful, you should still treat them as if they were helpful.

Putting all of your hopes on someone elevates that person to a position they can't possibly live up to. Many people set up expectations that are often too high. When contacts can't meet your expectations, it's foolish to blame them. That puts your energy in the wrong place.

"More important are your principles," says leadership expert Stephen Covey. "If you focus on what you're hoping to achieve rather than on people who failed to get you there as quickly as you liked, you're less likely to put pressure on those people. You don't want to ruin your relationship with them over your impatience. Always assume people who like you will do their best to help you, but don't expect a hundred percent as soon as you need it. It never happens, and you're just setting yourself up for disappointment.

"When you are at ease and let these people off the hook, it's amazing how open and optimistic you'll remain. Strive to be nurturing, sharing, and giving, no matter what happens."

CHAPTER ELEVEN

LUCKY SECRET 6:
Fireproof Your Bridges—
People Have Long Memories

A wise man will make more opportunities than he finds.

FRANCIS BACON

Lucky people view everyone they meet as a potential gatekeeper of opportunity. Who knows who could eventually be of help? We've all heard the horror stories about how the smallest insult screwed up someone's career and prevented them from getting a shot at what they wanted. Your reputation is key to your luck, but your reputation is worthless if you make enemies—either intentionally or unintentionally.

Watch Those Slights—You Could Get Burned

All it takes is one careless act that hurts someone's feelings to ruin your reputation and poison your luck. The worst part is you may never know how badly your offensive remarks may have hurt your chances of success. While you can't walk around constantly second-guessing everything you're about to say or do, you can never be too caring or sensitive about other people's feelings.

A senior executive at a *Fortune* 500 company in the South recently told me a startling story. A short time ago a woman was hired by her company at a level that was slightly lower than hers. The new person had been married just a few weeks before taking the job, so the senior executive sent the new woman a gift. Nothing extravagant—just a token of her warmth. The senior executive never received a note or a phone call of thanks. Two months went by. Then, one day, the senior executive and the woman were standing in the elevator alone. The senior executive turned to the woman and asked, "Gee, did the gift I sent you ever arrive? I never know whether or not things ever get to where they're going these days." The woman replied, "Oh, yes, I got it. Thank you so much."

Too little too late, and here's why: That afternoon the senior executive was in a meeting where she was asked her opinion of the new woman. The group was discussing promotions and job shifts. The senior executive was a powerful force among her peers and said flatly that the woman wasn't ready for more responsibility because her judgment wasn't good enough. So the job and substantial raise went to someone else who was equally qualified, and the woman's career was set back months if not years.

The moral of the story is that your luck can be thwarted if you aren't smart about how you do business. Did the woman mean to ignore the gratitude of the executive? Probably not. But her oversight and lack of grace cost her dearly. Was it nasty of the senior executive to factor in the woman's failure to send a thank-you note when considering the new woman's career? Absolutely not. If the newly hired woman didn't have the smarts to respond to the wedding gift in a mature, appropriate way, she probably wouldn't have been good at paying attention to details on the job. There's no excuse for a lack of manners, and such an oversight can spoil your luck for a long, long time.

But sometimes you get lucky and you get a second chance. Even in cases where you've hurt a powerful person's feelings, you can undo the damage by spotting the signs of pain early enough, tuning in to people who might know how the other person felt, and apologizing correctly. Many years ago a large meeting was held where I worked, and a rather controversial proposal was pitched by the head of the company. I didn't think it made sense, and when the group was asked for their opinions, I took the invitation literally and said why I didn't think it made sense. The head of the company's face went red and everyone else's went white.

After the meeting, a friend came up to me and mentioned that he thought that perhaps I should have disagreed differently—perhaps one-on-one in private. Angry, I asked why. "Because the head of the company was just in here and seemed insulted by what you said," he responded. I immediately went in to see the person and apologized, saying that my intention wasn't to embarrass him and that if I had it to do again, I would have seen him in private. From that day onward, we were on terrific terms.

How to fireproof your bridges . . .

• **Treat powerful people as if they were your boss—even if you don't work for them.** People with power have influence over people who can help you.

• **Take powerful people's initial reactions seriously.** Everyone reacts pretty much the same when they're insulted, at least in the beginning. Honest reactions come within the first few seconds, before people have a chance to mask up. Look for expressions of surprise or a tone that sounds as if they were caught off guard.

• **Always apologize in person or on the phone.** Never say you're sorry in writing. The spoken word is more meaningful in such situations. Your presence gives the person you've insulted a chance to see and hear you squirm, which always evens the score. Then it's over. For some reason, a written apology will be remembered far longer. You want your mistakes noted and then forgotten.

• **Always express your thanks in writing—and within days of receiving anything significant.** Whether it's in response to a gift, a raise, or a favor, there is nothing more powerful when it comes to gilding your reputation than a sincere and gracious note of thanks. Nothing.

• **Send a gift or flowers to your gatekeepers of opportunity when they've been especially helpful.** The expense is never a waste of money.

• **Never hesitate to do smart people a favor—even if your favor isn't immediately returned.** You'll always have a chance to call in your markers when you really need a break.

• **Never show your disappointment when someone smart or powerful has let you down.** Such displays of anger will always come as a surprise to them. They probably didn't intend to hurt you or fail to deliver. It's better for you to be a colleague or employee they can't remember than an enemy they can't forget.

Revenge Isn't Sweet—It's Dumb

Some people intentionally sever their links to key contacts. Usually their motive stems from feelings of outrage over being denied what they wanted, coupled with a burning desire to seek revenge. Exploding gives them more satisfaction than forgetting about the slight and protecting their image. They don't care about the long-term benefits of their reputation, only about the short-term satisfaction of hurting someone else.

Several years ago, someone I know who worked for a Broadway producer was passed over for a bigger position. He had been there for five years and had worked hard helping to promote the company's shows. But when one of his colleagues was promoted, he could barely contain his rage. He channeled that intense energy into networking, and within two months he had lined up another job at another theatrical production company. He gave just two weeks notice, even though the head of the company asked if he would stay on a few weeks longer until they got through a busy time. But this guy refused, telling others that the production company chief should have thought harder about promoting him. Two weeks later, he left.

The problem is that in the years that followed, many of this guy's colleagues moved on to other jobs and no one had a good word to say about him. Even though they sympathized with his situation at the time, everyone had the same opinion of him—that he was a reckless, overly emotional guy who probably would leave his company and colleagues in a lurch again. Had he departed with more grace, perhaps striking a deal with the head of the company, his name would have been held in higher regard and all of his bridges would have been intact. My friends tell me he was fired from his next job and is still looking for work.

The desire to strike back when you've been hurt is a natural reaction that can't really be suppressed. You can't ignore the wound, any more than you can ignore any other personal attack. When harnessed, such acrimonious feelings can be a positive force when they drive you to excel. They only become detrimental when you act out your fantasies of revenge.

A far more effective approach when you're hurt is to make the other person feel guilty. This will help you get what you want and keep you from unintentionally burning your bridges. A woman I know who worked for a Houston energy company was fired right after working hard to bring in business. She was a victim of the company's move to downsize in the early 1990s. Though tempted to make a fuss and if necessary sue, she decided to just go quietly.

But then she did something interesting. She stayed in contact with the person who had to let her go. She would send him articles and data that was important to his business and offer him positive advice in writing. She said she never once let on that she resented being fired or that she was having a tough time finding another position.

"I knew that eventually he would be able to help me, if only out of guilt," she said. "When you're let go due to staff cuts, no one likes to be the one to break the bad news. If you can find it in yourself to react graciously, you will elicit respect from those who had to lay you off. Two years later, my ex-boss introduced me to two other people who were starting their own company, and I joined as a third. I've never been happier."

Here's how to fireproof your bridges by letting powerful people off the hook and by not seeking revenge . . .

• **Always strive to be thought of as a class act by powerful people—even when you've been slighted or disappointed by them.** The more you take difficulties in stride and demonstrate your resilience, the more likely others will be to offer you opportunities in the future.

• **Resist the temptation to kick powerful people who have hurt you—even when *they're* down.** You're better off helping them up. No one likes cheap shots, not even the people who are on your side.

• **Make powerful people feel guilty about not offering you opportunities.** You do this by showering *them* with help and kindness. When they've slighted or ignored you, instead of rubbing it in, continue to assist them in any way possible. Eventually, their guilt will cause them to extend themselves when you need their help most.

• **Disappointments are always temporary.** Avoid thinking about them by using the time to come up with a plan to get back on track toward becoming lucky. Dwelling on disappointments only makes you bitter and curtails your luck-making abilities.

Bridges Are Slippery When You're Upset

Lucky people view every powerful person as a potential lifesaver—if not now, then eventually. A man I know who is the editor of a well-known magazine was in a jam a few years ago. At the time, he was editor of a magazine that was bought by another company. The new owners weren't easy to get along with, and they loved to micromanage everyone. This editor didn't appreciate having his creative freedom limited.

One day the magazine's public relations director called. A reporter for a trade magazine was coming in to profile the new owner. Did the editor want to be there to add color to the article? At first, my friend rejected this idea, sensing that he would look like a lap dog when the article came out. But the more he thought about it, the more he viewed the uncomfortable situation as an opportunity.

When the reporter came in, the editor was asked how he liked working for the new owner. He went on and on about how great it was and how much he was learning. When the article came out, industry executives could read between the lines, especially the part about "learning so much." His printed remarks were so unbelievably upbeat for someone who had to suffer such humiliation that they were interpreted as a sign that he must be on the verge of signing a big contract with the company or that he wanted out.

In retrospect, it would have been easy for this guy not to have cooperated with the interview by being conveniently at a meeting outside the office. It also would have been easy for him to provide a quote here or there to create the distinct impression in print that he wasn't completely happy working there.

"Look, I could have said to the reporter, 'I love working with the new owner. Sometimes we disagree over the editorial direction of the magazine, but we usually work it out.' That clearly would have been interpreted as, 'This guy is a pain in the ass, and I don't know how much longer I can put up with him.' But that kind of SOS doesn't get you great opportunities. It gets you pity. Instead, I made the new owner look good, which made me look good, and everything turned out great."

Within days after the article appeared, this guy's agent received four phone calls with job offers at other magazines—including one from a top editorial director who had previously turned him down for an earlier job. Today, he reports to that woman.

Why did the woman hire him after rejecting him in the past? Was it luck? Intrigued, he asked her those very questions at a lunch after she hired him. Here's what he told me she said: "When you submitted a proposal to me on how you'd change the magazine several years ago, there were two other people competing for the same job. Obviously, one of your two competitors got the job. But the other person whom I turned down was angry and never spoke to me again. You sent me a note thanking me for the opportunity and shrugged it off. Ever since that time, I've always had a high regard for you. It took a lot of character to view things that way."

What did my editor friend learn from both experiences?
Here's his advice for fireproofing your bridges and not doing
anything rash to spoil your luck . . .

• **Put on a happy face—even in difficult situations.** You'll look like a winner and people will want to steal you away for their team.

• **Don't wind up on important people's radar screens as a problem.** It is almost impossible to shake an impression that you're difficult to deal with or that you're hypersensitive. You're always better off forgetting about an insult and chalking it up to the other person's perception of reality, rather than reality itself.

• **Your biggest letdown is packed with opportunities.** Get over the hurt, and look for the rays of light in the darkened tunnel.

CHAPTER TWELVE

LUCKY SECRET 7:
Turn Small Triumphs into Lucky Streaks

All you need in life is ignorance and confidence,
and your success is assured.

MARK TWAIN

You are lucky when a high number of good things happen to you in short periods of time. For this phenomenon to occur, you must be able to convince lots of people that you're worth helping.

But getting people to help you once or a little isn't good enough. You want to take steps that maximize the frequency of that help and boost the quality. When this happens, you will have triggered a lucky streak. Lucky streaks have their own promotional values, and extending your luck requires that you be able to tell the golden opportunities from the unproductive ones. You then must have the guts to embrace the ones that stand the best chance of being the most helpful.

But you must be picky, or you run the risk of following too many questionable pieces of advice or chasing down too many false leads. It's far more productive to embrace only those challenges that will yield the best results and go farthest to bring you good fortune and make you look lucky. But you also want to experience good fortune over and over again, and within the shortest period of time. Triggering that chain reaction requires that you first know a few things about how lucky streaks work.

A lucky streak is a rapid succession of good fortune. But there must be progression too. Imagine boulders in a stream. To jump and land on one is good luck. To get to another is also good luck. But if you must jump far to each rock, the odds are great of falling in and not getting across. The trick is to find rocks that are close together so you reduce the odds of slipping as you move from one to the next. The closer together the rocks, the faster and drier you will arrive on the other side. When opportunities aren't close together, you must wait long periods of time for other opportunities or take bigger risks to find them. You lose your momentum, and the odds of losing your balance and slipping when you land are great.

When you seem to be able to quickly turn one lucky break into another, you have all but ensured your good fortune. As more seemingly lucky things happen to you, the sheer momentum of your good fortune will attract other people. You will also frighten off many of your rivals. People who make many good things happen over a short period of time are perceived as unstoppable, so most of your rivals and enemies will clear out of your way. They'll give up trying to derail you and become resigned to the fact that you are somehow blessed. How long your lucky streaks last depend largely on how big an impression your magic touch leaves on the people who can help and hinder you most.

Leaping Carefully into the Unknown

We face new challenges every day. Opportunities come up, and either we explore them or we don't bother. Some opportunities obviously are worth pursuing. But many others aren't so obvious, and they can have the biggest payoffs. To become luckier than you are now, you have to be able to spot the opportunities everyone else overlooks and show that you are capable of rising to embrace challenges.

Why do most people resist embracing challenges? Stephen Covey says that fear is a big factor. "Many people get 'grooved.' They become comfortable and complacent, and when an opportunity comes along they don't see it as an exciting challenge but as an obstacle. They lose their creative orientation.

"The energy you need to produce serendipity is really the natural consequence of a creative orientation rather than an ability to solve problems. A 'problem' is something we try to get rid of. But a creative orientation embraces problems to find the hidden opportunities. If you have a creative orientation, you will solve problems with the expectation of discovering new solutions. When problems emerge, you should have a 'by the way' reaction rather than 'I'm in trouble.' When you have a creative orientation toward life, your problems get solved not because you ignored them but because you approached them creatively."

Challenges are also frightening because the best ones force you to choose between what you have now and the unknown. A writer friend of mine who works as a reporter for a major newspaper was recently offered a position as a columnist at an on-line magazine. The opportunity paid well, but it meant giving up his newspaper job and embracing a challenge that might turn out to be the worst career move of his life.

Embracing challenges involves sacrifice at best and experiencing major setbacks at worst. The problem is that some people always imagine the worst when presented with challenges. It's a natural reaction. For example, my reporter friend declined the opportunity to write full-time for the magazine because he imagined himself miserable, cursing himself for ever giving up his newspaper job.

We all have these fatalistic views of the unknown. The trick is to change the way you see challenges and how you see yourself embracing them. The way to do this comfortably is to explore challenges at a comfortable, safe pace. If my reporter friend had tried to write a few on-line columns on a freelance basis to see how he liked it, he may have at least understood what he liked and disliked about the potential new position. He also would have made invaluable contacts.

From the perspective of the people who can make opportunities available to you over and over again, embracing challenges shows that you're out there swinging, that you are willing to take risks to improve your situation. More people will help you if you show that you aren't afraid to test the waters and to give the opportunities they offer you a shot. If you don't embrace challenges, the people who hold excellent opportunities won't be likely to present you with additional ones because they'll see you as someone who shies away from risk.

Embracing challenges also boosts your chances of meeting new people who can help you. Even when an opportunity does not work out, you almost always gain from the experience. I was once asked to give a half-hour speech at a conference of executive recruiters. I had never given a speech before, and the prospect scared me. I couldn't imagine standing in front of an audience and talking for an entire half hour. How could I write a speech that would hold people's interest for more than five minutes? I also worried, what if I make a mistake? Would I look like a jerk?

But as hard as giving a speech might be, I knew there would be a tremendous upside, even if I screwed up. At the very least, I would learn through the experience how *not* to give a speech. Or maybe I'd be good at it. Maybe people there would offer me opportunities in the future. In the end, I agreed to give the speech—and I did learn valuable lessons.

Did the speech generate offers of thousands of dollars to speak again? No. But I learned I could write and deliver a fairly amusing speech and do it pretty well. I knew that sometime in my life I would have to do it again, and now I had gotten that fear out of the way. I couldn't have learned the nuances of speech delivery and timing any other way. I also made several fabulous business contacts that I still keep up with to this day.

Smart Ways to Embrace the Right Challenges

The reason more people fail to embrace challenges is that they're afraid that they'll fail or be rejected. The status quo is a very safe, comfortable place to be, so challenges become viewed not as opportunities but as booby traps.

How can you teach yourself not to be afraid of challenges and to view them objectively? One way is to take ten minutes to think about the challenge at hand and imagine the worst-case scenario and the best-case scenario. If the best-case scenario sounds pretty good, deal with your fear directly by listing ways to minimize the risk of the worst happening.

Let's say, for example, that you get a call from someone who offers you an opportunity to make some extra money in your spare time working on a project. The upside is the money, of course, and the contacts you may meet along the way. If the people with whom you work on the project are smart and well-connected, they will share even better opportunities with you if you do a good job and turn in your work on time without much fuss. The worst-case scenario is that your life will become more hectic, your family and friends may see you less, and you'll have to spend much of your free time working. There's also the risk of not getting paid when you had hoped to, of the need to do revisions, and that nothing good may come of the assignment.

At this point, we usually add everything up and ask ourselves: Is it worth it? I've found that in almost every case, a challenge is worth it if the money is right and the people involved know what they're doing. Whenever I decide to embrace a challenge, I think through ways to minimize my biggest fears.

In the case of the spare-time project, for example, you can ask to submit a project in thirds. This way the project is more likely to be approved along the way—or, if any revisions are necessary, they can be done in more manageable stages. You can insist on a contract that guarantees partial payments along the way. You can carefully organize your time so that you can get more done and so that your time isn't wasted. If, when you're done, your solutions have addressed most of your fears, go for it.

Here are other strategies that the lucky people I know use to embrace challenges . . .

• **Think of challenges as learning curves, not hairpin turns.** Everyone fears the unknown, and every challenge is a little scary. Yet some people successfully replace that anxiety with eager anticipation and take the plunge. Instead of imagining the worst, they tell themselves, "No matter what happens, I'll learn something from this experience." And the truth is, you will. Embracing challenges is always intimidating at first. But once you realize you're not going to go off a cliff, that you're going to survive, you become wiser and stronger from the experience, even if embracing the challenge was a mistake.

A successful photographer I know who specializes in shooting celebrities for glossy magazines told me she always used to get nervous when she got an assignment. "I would always start imagining the worst—that my film would be poorly exposed or lost. I literally felt ill before going on assignment. That changed a bunch of years ago, when

I photographed a famous singer. The editor wanted something different, some sort of tension that would show how popular the performer was. But when I arrived at the theater where the person was rehearsing, I was given only fifteen minutes with the guy—and the photo shoot had to take place on stage.

I started to get really scared—the kind of scared where you freeze up. I suddenly realized I had a choice. I could take charge of the photo shoot fast, or return with lousy pictures. So I embraced the situation. I screamed for all of the roadies and tech people I could find to stand behind the guy on the different risers that were set up for the musicians. There were about fifty people back there crowded together. I shot him close, with the crowd standing at different levels, a little out of focus.

When I delivered the film, the editor loved them. Looking at the photos, you couldn't tell why all those people were standing at different levels in the background, which gave the photos drama. It created this surreal audience backdrop. When the photo appeared, the performer liked it so much that I did his next album cover. Now when photo editors call at the last minute, I can't wait to find solutions to problems on the fly. I've replaced my fears with the memory of that successful fifteen-minute shoot. I've learned to think of fear as my intuition telling me to go for it. Believe me, it works."

• **You're only in competition with yourself.** If you spend your energy just battling your rivals, you won't embrace challenges nor will you attract opportunity. Focusing your energy on becoming smarter, more efficient, and more creative than you were six months ago is harder than trying to outlast your competition. Forcing others to underperform is easy, but you learn very little from the exercise. When you are in competition with yourself, challenges are your sole means of improving yourself and you will view them as opportunities, not as high-stakes gambles that will cause you pain or setbacks.

Competing with yourself isn't about seeing yourself as the center of the world. Such an egocentric attitude alienates more people than it attracts. When you compete with yourself, you actually become less antagonistic and less aggressive around other people. Your rivals no longer matter and you don't have to clash with them. If you do what you do well, and strive to do it better in six months or a year, you stand the best chance of attracting opportunity. Your efforts will be recognized and no one will be offended by your behavior.

When you are more concerned about the quality of your work than about how you stack up against other people, you reach a very peaceful state. Hostility, anger, and all of the other emotions that work against your good fortune vanish, and more people will want to reward you for your efforts.

• **Take challenges for a test drive before embracing them.** One of the luckiest people I know is brilliant at embracing challenges. He now heads a major cable-TV network. Despite having extremely poor eyesight, he always has held top media jobs. He is a master of detail and is loaded with magnetism and energy. Anyone who has ever worked with him has been motivated to do their best work. One of his secrets is finding something special about everyone and deferring to each person's passion and expertise. Because of his poor vision, he surrounds himself with people who are fanatics, and he relies on their judgment.

When I worked with him, he gave me a piece of advice that still rings in my head: "Don't worry about the difficulty of any challenge, so long as you can fake it for a while. Soon after taking on the challenge, you're going to meet the person who knows all the details of your job and will help guide you. That person exists in every situation I've ever been in. You will always come out ahead, no matter what challenge you face. Just look for the guide."

A very Zen-like approach, but it has worked for him. No matter what top positions in magazines and TV he has held, the jobs never required the same set of skills. Soon after landing one, he would set to work finding the person who knew all the players and how everything worked. "In almost every case," he said, "this person was someone who had been pushed aside and forgotten and was just waiting for the chance to shine again." He would make this person a loyal member of his team by trusting the person's instincts rather than by telling him or her what to do.

He can also be gruff and decisive. "I'm that way only when I feel there is nonsense resistance to what I want to do—opposition that's based on office politics, not common sense. Not being able to see well unless it's inches from my face gives me a big advantage. My other senses are stronger, and so are my intuition and instincts."

This person taught himself to enjoy learning on the job, a prospect that would frighten even most people with perfect eyesight. Each opportunity in his career has been a new adventure, not a lateral move. "If I've done it before, I don't want to do it again," he said. How can you be sure that a challenge is worthwhile? "Ask great questions. Before I take on any challenge, I spend days coming up with dozens of questions. Then I cut the list down to five big ones. Before I embrace any challenge, I want to know whether I'm going to be able to get the resources I'll need or be able to hire the right talent, and whether my ideas will be well-received."

• **Deal with fear as you would a bully**. Fear is a product of your imagination. Sometimes it's smart to be afraid. Long ago, that instinct kept us from being eaten by tigers. But in most cases, fear is nothing more than your emotional side convincing you not to make life too difficult for yourself.

If you think of fear as an emotional bully and adapt the attitude that bullies must be confronted, then you won't allow yourself to be pushed around by fear. The worst that can happen is that the challenge you face will be a bad move. But I guarantee you will learn from it—and make new friends who will be helpful later on.

How to Create Lucky Streaks

Lucky streaks are triggered by an abundance of opportunities. To coax a lucky streak into motion, you have to find ways to increase the volume of good fortune that comes your way. You do this by parlaying one opportunity into another. Every opportunity must be viewed not as a single, isolated event but as a staging platform for the next opportunity. Your mindset when an opportunity comes along shouldn't be, "Great! This is the answer to my prayers," but, "Great, now let's see how I can turn this opportunity into other ones."

Here are the secrets of lucky people who turn opportunities into lucky streaks . . .

• **Think dimensionally about opportunities.** Many people think of the struggle to get what they want as a series of individual battles that must be fought and won, one at a time. But if you think this way, you are likely to rest on each step, waiting for someone to help you. Sometimes that happens, but most of the time that person never arrives. In reality, one person rarely can make all of your dreams come true, and a single opportunity rarely gives you everything you want.

But if you think dimensionally—looking at the many possibilities that exist in any situation—you're more likely to create multiple opportunities. "So many people think their capacity is limited," says Stephen Covey. "They're unaware they have eight cylinders. They can be involved in many creative projects at the same time. I always think in terms of satisfying all of my roles—as a business person, as a lecturer, and as a father. I think about what I would like to accomplish in each of those roles. This enlarges my mental and spiritual capacity and allows me to see myself as capable and not overwhelmed. When people think this way, happy accidents emerge from the interfaces of those many roles."

When you're able to think on many different levels at once, you won't be satisfied with one opportunity or one triumph. Every opportunity will be viewed as two halves—one half to be enjoyed now and the other to be used to produce new ones. Summon the same courage to meet those challenges over and over until you have what you want.

• **Clone your opportunities.** The more opportunities that come your way, the faster you'll get what you want, especially if those opportunities move you toward a specific goal. The best way to boost your opportunities is to ask for them. Most of us hesitate to do so when we meet someone for the first time, or after someone has already given us an opportunity. Lucky people don't live by these rules. They are only interested in generating as many opportunities as possible in the shortest amount of time.

I have a friend whom people love to help. No matter whom I introduce to this person, I learn later that my friend has asked for contacts and other favors. She's direct about it, and that approach works for her. She isn't shy about asking for invitations, and she isn't shy about helping other people. At first I thought it was really forward of her. But the people she asked never complained or felt exploited.

"Look, life is like darts," she says. "I guarantee that if I give you one dart and tell you to throw it at the board, chances are slim that you'll hit the bull's eye. But if I give you five darts, your chances are going to increase tremendously—even if you throw them all at once. In other words, the more people you have helping you reach your goal, the more likely you are to get what you want fast, or at least close to it. Luck is impatient."

My friend's rules are simple: Ask everyone you meet three questions about what they want and tell them three things you want. She calls this "three in, three out," and she says it always produces opportunities. She recently asked someone she met at a party, "What do you do for a living? What do you want most at work and outside of work? And how can I help you get what you want?" The person gave her three answers, and my friend had three contacts for the person to call.

Then she told the woman three things that she wanted: "I'm looking for a great contractor to renovate my kitchen, I'm looking to hire a great number-two at work, and my sister is looking to meet someone cute." The woman was able to help her with two of the three. Was the guy cute? Not really, but he could have been. The contractor was great, however, and did a fabulous job on her kitchen. He even knew a great landscaper.

• **Be a momentum player.** Wherever there are people, there are opportunities. Whether you choose to engage those people or not is up to you. To keep the opportunities coming, you can't be shy. If you can't be outgoing in person, work the phones. If you can't work the phones, write. Whatever it takes, you have to stay in touch with as many people as possible if you want to parlay one opportunity into the next. Keep a month-at-a-glance planner just for names of luck-makers with whom you should touch base. Then push for lunch and talk about what the other person is up to.

"When you're an independent contractor," a freelance writer told me recently, "you're dependent on the goodwill of others. By staying in touch with about twenty-five different contacts, I always have work coming in. The reason I call my contacts regularly is because it's easy to fall off their lists and easy to be forgotten. My aim is to always have work, and that takes great contacts and lucky streaks. I cut down on the volatility of those streaks by staying in touch. Even if I play phone tag with contacts for a week, I've succeeded in reminding them that I'm here and that I'm thinking of them. The name of the game is to be on contacts' minds as often as possible."

• **Act surprised by your good fortune.** Lucky streaks speak for themselves. When you're on a roll, people know it. They're amazed by your ability to always land on your feet, or that you always wind up on top.

That's why you must never explain how you micromanage your lucky streaks. You have to make your good fortune seem as big a mystery to you as it is to others. Like great magicians, you can't reveal the secrets of your tricks. Your gains have to look as if you're doing very little to attract opportunities, even though you're really actively parlaying one opportunity into the next. The more puzzled people are by your good fortune, the more they'll assume that you're "blessed," and the more likely they'll be to offer you work, contracts, opportunities, and rewards.

To be the recipient of good luck is wonderful. But if you can boost the frequency of that luck, you'll be doubly lucky and you will be twice as likely to get what you want in half the time. One of the country's foremost experts on mutual funds is brilliant at creating lucky streaks and then acting amazed by it all. I know how hard he crunches numbers and studies the results to come up with great advice for clients and the media. The more he publicly dismisses his amazing track record, the more clients he picks up.

I asked him how he makes luck and parlays one opportunity into the next. "There are two things I learned long ago: Master the hardest part of your specialty and you'll do better than most of the people in your field. So if I played tennis, I'd master my backhand and the most difficult backhand shot. The other is to make sure you're the first to act surprised by your repeated success. It will make you lucky every time."

PART THREE

HOW TO LIMIT BAD LUCK

Lots of folks confuse bad management with destiny.

ANONYMOUS

Now that you know how lucky people improve their good fortune, the next step is to master their skills for minimizing bad luck. Learning these secrets isn't optional. No matter how good you are at getting people to give you what you want, your efforts will be wasted unless you can reduce your mistakes and do damage control. Negative behavior can spoil lucky streaks. So can poor judgment.

■ CHAPTER THIRTEEN ■

Gaining Control Over Bad Luck

Luck is a matter of preparation meeting opportunity.
OPRAH WINFREY

As we now know, making luck requires specific behavior skills. But to keep good luck coming, you need to be able to play defense as well as offense. To get what you want in life, you must master both. Good luck doesn't stick around when bad luck strikes, and bad luck rarely leaves in a hurry. When you're hit with misfortune, opportunities dry up, the people you thought were close friends don't return calls, and life gets a lot harder. How long your good luck lasts depends on how well you manage misfortune.

Bad Luck Isn't Your Fault—Or Is It?

We view good luck and bad luck very differently. When we experience good luck, we think of all the things we had to do to make that good luck happen. Bad luck, however, is always viewed as the mysterious work of external forces. Bad luck is an "act of God," the result of people or supernatural forces conspiring against us, or anything else that isn't within our control. We resist holding ourselves responsible for our own misfortune because the thought that we might have had something to do with our bad luck is too painful.

But not facing up to the fact that your behavior and judgment play big roles in how much misfortune you encounter promotes scapegoat logic and irresponsibility. The more you make excuses for difficulties that arise, the more likely you are to ignore the actions you could have taken to better influence your luck. When you fail to sufficiently think through decisions or you blame others for the problems you face, you likely will make the same mistakes again and again.

This attitude will also fool you into believing that you are always right. Blaming circumstances or others for your misfortune makes you feel good because your self-esteem is able to hide safely behind the facade you've created. But while finger-pointing is comforting, casting yourself as a martyr rarely improves your luck. You become a less attractive candidate for help because you come across as someone who doesn't take responsibility. Playing the role of innocent victim leads us to feel sorry for ourselves, but few people find self-pity pretty or alluring.

While you cannot completely control the random events that surround you, many of the problems you face can be avoided or at least minimized. Even when misfortune strikes, there are steps you can take to speed its departure or overrun it with good luck. It all boils down to the choices we make. Most people who encounter a disproportionately high amount of bad luck have one thing in common: They have a hard time controlling behavior that attracts trouble. Seemingly determined to repeat the same mistakes over and over, these people can't remember—or refuse to remember—what it was that reduced people's opinions of them or why people stopped helping them. Egotism or ignorance keep them from heeding the warning signs that are obvious to others, and they continue to inflame those around them.

We all know people who irritate the people who deal with them. They appear to be chronically unable to learn from their mistakes. They create negative impressions and large amounts of ill will. They stubbornly believe their approaches are the right ones and that everyone else can't appreciate their genius. Because of this attitude and narrow outlook, they suffer more bad luck. The fact is, life does not have to be so difficult. You'll find life much more rewarding if you improve your judgment just a little bit.

Judgment's Role in Limiting Bad Luck

Before we act, we think. What we think about determines the quality of our judgment. If your deliberations successfully predict how your actions will affect other people, and you fashion your behavior to minimize the fallout, your judgment is considered pretty good. If you can't accurately predict the repercussions of your actions—or you choose to ignore your predictions—your judgment is going to be poor.

The thinking process that takes place before decisions are made is heavily influenced by our past experiences, common sense, and, to some degree, fear. That's why our decisions are sometimes flawed and fail to produce what we expect. Good judgment requires that we ask ourselves two fundamental questions before we act: What can I say or do that will help me get what I want . . . and what impact will my actions have on others. Unfortunately, most people do very little reflecting or projecting before they act—or they answer one question but not the other.

People who are concerned only with short-term satisfaction tend to act impulsively. They do whatever makes them feel good, with little regard for how their behavior might make other people feel or react. On the other hand, people who are preoccupied only with how their actions will affect others usually neglect their own desires and wishes.

They respond to situations by trying to please other people, without taking into consideration what *they* truly want. Both types—those who impulsively think only of themselves, and those who instinctively think only of others—are not exercising the best judgment. Therefore, they're both much more liable to attract bad luck than the people who carefully consider how their actions will affect both their own desires and the responses of others.

To predict with any accuracy how well or how poorly your behavior will be received, you must teach yourself to identify potential problems in advance and take steps to avoid them. If you behave in ways that anger other people or make them lose respect for you, you will invite bad luck. You risk permanently turning people against you when you act without asking yourself what impact your actions will have on others. Of course, you can't make everyone respect and love you all of the time. But you can protect your good luck by limiting how much bad luck you create through flawed decision making.

We all know people who are annoying because they behave without any regard for our space or feelings. They say whatever comes into their heads and they act impulsively, regardless of who is offended. Sometimes it pays to behave impulsively, but the more we think through what we're about to say and do, the better our decisions will be and the fewer people will want to stand in our way. The more conscious you are of the possible scenarios that are likely to follow your behavior, the lower your risk of choosing one that draws a negative response.

Much of our bad luck with people is controllable—or at least manageable—if we can improve our judgment just a little bit. By becoming more aware of how others are likely to feel or react as a consequence of what you say or do, your decisions will be better, you'll be more respected, and you will be more handsomely rewarded.

Good judgment won't necessarily improve your luck, but it will limit the amount of bad luck you're likely to experience. Hold your bad luck down, and whatever you do to make good luck happen will have more power because there will be less resistance from others.

How to Improve Your Judgment

Good judgment helps you steer clear of people and situations that can damage your luck. To improve your judgment, you first must believe that getting what you ultimately want in life is more important than saying and doing whatever you please. Expecting people to tolerate and forgive whatever you say or do is shortsighted and foolish. Far more powerful and gratifying in the long term is thinking through the consequences of your behavior before you act. If you can accurately anticipate the potential for resistance and rejection, your decisions will create fewer problems for you.

"You stand a much better chance of succeeding and attracting opportunity if you actively take steps to reduce the number of mistakes you make," says Martin Edelston, president of Boardroom Inc. "To do that, you have to make better decisions. First you need to learn as much as you can about the issues involved. Then you must carefully think through what outcome is in your best interests and how others will react to you. Only then does it make sense to move forward. Once you know what you want to accomplish, all of your decisions will become easier.

"To become thoroughly informed about the issues you're facing, you should read as much as you can and listen to as many knowledgeable people as possible before acting.

"I learned this when I was in my teens. I was on the high school cross-country team—the worst one on the team. By reading the few books on running that were available then, I was able to improve and become one of the best long-distance runners in New Jersey. Through acquired knowledge, I was able to make decisions about my training and technique that significantly improved my performance. The miracle of my success as a runner helped me realize that I could apply the same tenacity and do the same type of research to excel at nearly everything.

"Only after you've done your homework can you plan strategy. It also pays to talk out loud—either to yourself or to others—about the big decisions you must make. You need to hear yourself think. Peter Drucker, the management guru, was once asked why he talked so much. His answer was, 'Because I learn so much when I speak.' Talking helps you bring out what's inside you—to recognize every issue's many sides—and it allows you to rationalize your actions."

Here's what the other people I know with good judgment do
to keep their decision-making skills sharp . . .

• **Think about the impact of your actions.** Everything you say and do has a negative, positive, or neutral impact on other people. Insult everyone with whom you speak, and you'll make a lot of enemies. Position what you say or do in ways that make people feel good or neutral about you, and you'll clear the way for good luck.

The key to better judgment is thinking through the consequences of your actions. The reason we don't drop a glass on the floor is that we know the glass will break, there will be lots of little pieces, it will be hard to clean up, and someone may step on a piece we've missed and get hurt. That's consequential thinking. Now try to use the same type of consequential thinking when you're considering specific behavior or actions.

If you determine that your behavior will make a large number of important people angry or upset, change your plan of action. Consequential thinking isn't a plan of appeasement. It's just a matter of thinking before acting. You may decide after you think about it that the least popular approach makes the most sense and that you're willing to risk attracting bad luck. That's fine. Consequential thinking is merely the process of determining the stakes. Once you have a pretty good idea of the outcome, you're prepared for the fallout. When you're prepared, you can take steps to control the damage. When you're not prepared, you're more likely to use poor judgment when making additional decisions, which can result in even more bad luck.

People who are particularly smooth at consequential thinking
ask themselves a series of questions before they speak or act . . .

- **Do I have to respond or act immediately?**
- **How will taking more time help me in this situation?**
- **If I act now, what exactly do I want to say or do?**
- **Who will be affected by my remarks or actions?**
- **Who will be offended?**
- **Does it matter if they're offended?**
- **How can I refine my remarks or actions to offend the least number of people?**
- **If I cannot avoid hurting people, what can I do on the back end to ease their pain?**

- **Learn to read people better.** Judgment is about coming to smart conclusions before you act. But it's also about anticipating how others will respond. This requires an ability to put yourself in other people's shoes, to imagine what they might feel. Such sensitivity requires that you be able to put yourself second and other people first. Again, you may decide in the final analysis that what you must say or do overrides their needs. Still, the fact that you thought about how your behavior will affect others reduces your chances of attracting bad luck.

What about situations where you don't know the people you're dealing with and you aren't sure how they'll react to you? Certainly, you can use common sense and past experiences. But it also helps to know a little bit about human behavior. "The fastest way to learn about human behavior is to sit back, shut up, and study the people you're dealing with," a psychiatrist friend told me.

"I don't care whether it's a first date or a business meeting. Instead of being the first one to talk or act, watch how the people are behaving and interacting with each other. Are they nervous? Why are they nervous? Do they feel threatened? Is there tension in the room? Why? And why did the person who just spoke say what he or she said? Could they have positioned what they said differently? Don't be the first to act or talk. First ask yourself, 'Who in the room is a true friend and who are potential foes?' Then you need to position what you want to say or do in a way that will put most people at ease. Developing that kind of sensitivity will always improve your judgment and reduce bad luck. You're always better erring on the side of hesitation and moderation than recklessness and impulsiveness."

• **Consider the downside of every problem.** People who speak and act without thinking first are convinced they are right and everyone else is wrong. When you fail to think about problems from all sides, you neglect to factor in the worst-case reactions to your behavior. Not having this information prevents you from considering that your behavior may have negative implications.

Limit your bad luck by making sure the worst doesn't happen. Before you act, work through the worst-case scenarios. If the worst that can happen is indeed an extremely negative outcome for you, work backward to find ways of handling the situation that will produce different results. Even if the worst does happen, you'll be prepared to put another plan into action and control the damage.

• **Pick your moments.** Poor judgment isn't always about saying or doing the wrong thing. Sometimes it's about saying or doing the right thing—but at the wrong time. We've all been in situations where someone says something that makes perfect sense but is irritatingly inappropriate. Perhaps we became angry when what was said came as a complete surprise to us. Or perhaps what was said in an open meeting would have been better received had it been taken up with us individually. Or maybe we were just not in the mood to hear it.

Good judgment requires good timing. A corporate attorney I know tests her timing by running her ideas by smaller audiences first. "I call it 'previewing,'" she says. "I won't introduce controversial ideas at large meetings unless I've first had a chance to pre-sell them to each person who will attend. I'm particularly interested in individual reactions to what I'm saying. If there's resistance, I want to know why. I listen for their reactions. If they recommend against it or they are unsure, I usually decide to postpone what I wanted to say until I can figure out how to introduce it another way."

Another person I know waits until everyone else at the meeting has had a chance to speak or has loosened up. "You have to know your audience," he says. "When people are comfortable, they're more likely to listen objectively to what you're saying. I'm careful to know when to drop what I'm pushing. It's easy to get so caught up in your own ideas that you can't sense when people are no longer interested or when they're irritated. When I sense a disconnect, I immediately say, 'Maybe I'm wrong. What do you think?' The question brings others back into the conversation, and doesn't leave them with a bad feeling about me or what I've said or done."

• **Learn to apologize.** Even smart people make bad decisions. You think you're doing the right thing, but it doesn't always work out that way. While it's impossible to fully predict how your behavior will be received, you have to move fast when it's clear that people have misread your intentions. All it takes is one disgruntled person to start an avalanche of misfortune.

One of the best ways to undo a bad decision is to apologize. I'm always amazed how hard it is for most people to say they are sorry. I suppose, in part, it's because they are stubborn, or they put their pride ahead of good judgment. The way to apologize so that your luck improves is to do it behind the scenes and one-on-one.

Apologizing publicly is almost always a sign of poor judgment. You're putting your image on the line, and a tarnished image can ruin your luck. Also, a public apology is almost always unnecessary. An apology is most potent when it's heartfelt. And here's a bonus: Rather than make you seem weak and unlucky, a personal apology will almost always boost your image with the person and improve your luck.

■ CHAPTER FOURTEEN ■

Get Over It

No man thinks clearly when his fists are clenched.

ANONYMOUS

Dissatisfaction, disappointment, and disrespect are the three main reasons why we become angry. It feels good to show hostility when we are frustrated, hurt, or need to get what we want. The problem is that while anger feels good—allowing us to let off steam—it almost always creates great potential for bad luck.

You become lucky and stay lucky by gaining control of your temper. You can't let people walk all over you, but how you register your unhappiness is critical. The better able you are to control yourself, the more you'll be respected. Anger never convinces people to go out of their way for you or to create opportunities for you. Instead, it pushes people away. Victims of your anger will likely seek revenge, either on their own or by helping your enemies. The people who witness or hear about your hostility will think your behavior is erratic and that you're someone to avoid. No one I know was ever given a great opportunity because of his or her temper.

Why Anger Limits Luck

Losing your temper and blasting people feels justified because we believe they deserved it. But blowing your cool also makes people afraid of you and discourages them, and everyone who saw or heard you, from offering you opportunities.

The other problem with anger is that it's highly addictive behavior. Once you express yourself in a charged, emotional way, the sensation of stress leaving your body feels so good that it's tempting to release hostility this way the next time you feel it. Tension strikes or we become displeased, and rather than catch ourselves, we release our pent-up animosity. The angrier we are, the less good luck comes our way, and the more bitter we become. It's a vicious cycle. Think of the bitter people you know. Fewer good things happen to them and they resent their misfortune, which they then express by lashing out, which reduces their luck yet again.

When I started working in the *New York Times'* sports department in the early 1980s, there were some really tough deputy editors working there. They had no self-control and regularly chewed out reporters, copy editors, and copyboys in the newsroom for all to see and hear. When you caught hell for a mistake, you really felt worthless.

To survive those public hazing sessions without breaking down, you had to have tremendous self-discipline. You had no choice. You were at their mercy, and everyone knew it was a privilege to work there. Explosive editors were universally hated in the department and nearly everyone secretly wished these guys would be transferred or fired. Over the course of a few years, that's exactly what happened. The hot-tempered editors all lost major power struggles and were forced out. They had no allies, and their own performance was undercut because they didn't get the best out of the people who worked for them.

When you display your temper, you are walking a high wire without a net. You have no support, no one to look out for you, no one to tell you about a problem that's heading your way, and no one to help you avoid trouble before it arrives. If you torment enough people, not only will you have nothing to protect your fall but people will start shaking the poles that are holding the wire on which you're walking in an attempt to ensure your tumble.

When to Express Anger . . . and When to Hide Your Cards

Certainly there's a time and place for outrage. If you see cruelty or injustice, expressing displeasure in the most strident way is completely appropriate. Anger is also appropriate in cases where it serves as a warning to people who repeatedly try to take advantage of you. Sometimes severity is the only way to get someone's attention or respect.

In other cases, anger must be expressed first before you can start communicating. Keeping rage bottled up inside can lead to personal vendettas and feuds, which always wind up destroying the reputations of all parties involved. But anger can be expressed calmly. When issues are discussed rationally, people understand each other and they start to forgive.

And then there are going to be times when you simply lose your cool. We've all been there. You're under stress, people annoy you, and you lose it. Everyone blows a fuse from time to time. Such occasional outbursts are accepted and usually excused.

It's only when anger becomes standard operating procedure that it becomes dangerous to your luck. Anger can also derail your good fortune when it's expressed at an inappropriate time.

Here are instances when it's never smart to express your anger . . .

- **when you hold the upper hand but could lose your advantage if you become angry**

- when your anger clearly is based on ego and self-interest rather than on improving standards
- when the person at whom you're going to get angry could help you in the future
- when your anger won't produce results, just a sense of personal relief and satisfaction
- when word of your outburst will likely get around and tarnish your reputation
- when you find yourself regularly getting angry at someone who annoys you but is helpless, thus casting you in the role of bully

How to Get Angry without Destroying Your Luck

I know how hard it is to control anger. I knew many artists while growing up who freely expressed their rage. The excuse they had was that it was part of their artistic, creative force. But I also saw how debilitating that anger could be. Anger limited their opportunities because they viewed it as an asset rather than a liability. You turn off so many people with your rage that your luck just dries up. Life becomes a lot harder—much harder than it has to be.

*Here are the secrets of lucky people who get angry
in a positive way . . .*

• **Be assertive and coy, rather than hostile and rude.** Professional poker champ Barbara Enright knows there's a big difference between being assertive and being hostile. "I would rather enrage opponents than become enraged," she says. "You see, there's a big difference between being assertive and being obnoxious. At the poker table, being assertive is about you and your aggressive style of play. The object is winning, and everyone uses every trick in the book to psyche out opponents. But being hostile and obnoxious involves personal attacks, and such behavior always inflames opponents rather than psyching them out. When opponents are inflamed, your luck is almost sure to decline.

"Hostility involves cruelty, and when you're hostile, hurting opponents becomes your goal, not winning the game. Being hostile only makes your opponent try harder to beat you, which ruins your luck. When you feel anger coming on, you're too caught up emotionally in the game. To win, you need to think, 'Why am I reacting this way?' The answer is always to ignore it, to walk away."

• **Recognize that the people who make you mad are often playing a game.** Everyone plays games to some extent. We all want something, and we all do things and sacrifice things to get it. When people irritate us, it is usually because their mind game is triggering negative behavior. Some people always arrive late or neglect to prepare for meetings. You can get angry, but you'll be better able to get a grip if you view their behavior as a game. Their lateness has nothing to do with you personally. Address the problem if it bothers you. Just don't do it in a way that raises the stakes emotionally or tarnishes your image.

How can you show displeasure without losing your cool? "The thing that makes me crazy is when I ask someone a question and they smugly try to make my question seem inconsequential or silly," says top money manager Michael Stolper. "They're afraid to say they don't know the answer or they try to dump the problem back in my lap. When this happens, instead of losing it, I say, 'This is really annoying. We're going in circles. Is there some other way we can get this solved and move on?' This question always gives me distance, which keeps me from taking their remarks personally. It also makes them look unprofessional without putting my own image or reputation in jeopardy."

• **Know when to hit the eject button.** Before any damage is done, you're better off disengaging than becoming hostile. When you feel anger swelling, either get up and leave or tell yourself you're checking out emotionally. Don't feel as if you have to stay and fight. Know yourself well enough to get out of the situation before it explodes. Between your anger and an outburst is a bubble—a space of a few seconds in which you can get a grip before you crack. When you feel your anger rising, you want the other person to pay an emotional price for his or her behavior. Rage starts to push up through your chest until you're on the verge of blasting the person. Just at this point you must catch yourself. Rather than let the bubble burst and satisfy your desire to punish the person, you have to leave the meeting emotionally. Think about what you're planning to do on the weekend, or start making lists of things you need to do later that day. If you can catch yourself before your emotional bubble bursts, your anger will dissipate. You will have ejected.

Taking Risks, Making Mistakes, and Bouncing Back

Misery loves company, and the longer you dwell on your misfortune, the more bad luck you're likely to experience. Agonizing over actions you should or shouldn't have taken always leads to self-doubt and complaining, which compromises your judgment and stains your lucky reputation.

Disappointment rarely gives much warning. Letdowns strike unexpectedly and always leave us wondering whether we could have done anything to prevent them and what we can do differently in the future. It's smart to analyze what role you played in creating misfortune and what steps, if any, you could have taken to prevent it. Reflecting on life's disappointments helps you discover clever ways to improve your luck.

How fast you are able to work through this self-evaluation and move on with your life dictates the quality of your luck. If you dwell on your setbacks and obsess over your actions, you will experience more bad luck. You need to learn from your mistakes and move on. View mistakes not as permanent injuries to your self-esteem but as temporary pain that time will wash away. If you do this, your mind will return quickly to the process of assessing challenges and risk rather than dwelling on errors and blowing them out of proportion.

No matter how clever you are, you're going to make mistakes. If you're not making mistakes periodically, you're probably not taking enough risk, and you'll never make good luck happen if you don't take risks. Limiting bad luck is about striking a balance between risk and reward. With every effort, there have to be reasonably good odds of gaining what you set out to achieve versus losing what you now posses.

Don't confuse risk with recklessness. Risk is about calculation and sizing up the odds before taking chances. Reckless behavior is the absence of calculation. If your actions are driven by desperation, you're acting out of recklessness. Instead of weighing your chances of success, you're acting out of impulse, and you will likely make the same mistakes repeatedly.

"Before I act on anything where the outcome isn't certain," says money manager Michael Stolper, "I always ask myself, 'What will happen if what I'm about to do is a mistake? What will it cost me in time, in money, in fear, and in anxiety?' The anxiety part is what I call the 'neurosis factor.' If my venture turns out to be a mistake, I need to know how I can fix it. It's also important to ask yourself, 'If my venture is a mistake, can I get out of it?' Sometimes you can get tethered to a problem, forcing you to pay a huge emotional price trying to extricate yourself from it. I look for opportunities that provide a big benefit with the least amount of anxiety."

The neurosis factor can also cause you to overdramatize your mistakes and see life as unfair. That's why you're better off thinking about your setbacks as individual instances of miscalculation rather than a giant conspiracy to get you. Only then will you realize that mistakes aren't evil, they're just a natural part of risk taking and getting lucky.

Secrets of Bouncing Back

An important difference between people who are lucky and people who aren't is the amount of time it takes for them to get over disappointment. We all know people who don't seem to be affected when hit by setbacks or misfortune. We also know people who crumple up at the slightest letdown. No one likes to obsess over problems and mistakes, but only a few are able to liberate themselves quickly and move on to make more luck.

Here are some of the things lucky people tell themselves
when unexpected setbacks strike . . .

• **What I'm worrying about is silly—it matters more to me than to others.** We all become paralyzed when we're disappointed or rejected. When we're down on our luck, the image we have of ourselves is shattered and we feel like failures.

Lucky people occasionally feel that way too, but for a shorter period of time than everyone else. They are able to move on, refusing to process mistakes or disappointments as major failures or tragedies. "Of course I make mistakes—big ones," a successful, lucky friend in the fashion industry told me. "My biggest fear isn't of the mistake itself or how I'll look to others. It's that the mistake is going to make me feel sorry for myself. When that happens, it's over. I'm terrified of feeling sorry for myself. You never recover once that starts.

"I recover by telling myself two things: 'I did the best I could, so that's the way it goes,' and, 'If I can't have it, I don't want it.' You've got to tell yourself these things quickly, right after you've screwed up or have been let down. Then you have to focus on other things and let time clean and heal your wound. The reality is always that your mistake or setback isn't nearly as big as you think it is, and it's always smaller than someone else's problems at that moment somewhere else in the world.

"Mistakes and setbacks can't hurt you—only the way in which you react to them. If you act like a jerk, people are going to think you're a jerk and lose confidence in you. Don't feel sorry for yourself, and other people won't either."

• **Mistakes are part of every process.** I've been lucky to work with highly successful people. Knowing these people as well as I do has given me an up-close look at how they interpret and deal with mistakes. It's their ability to shake off mistakes that allows them to rise to such lofty positions of power. They are ready for the emotional turmoil that mistakes and disappointment bring. They see both as part of the weather conditions that exist at their elevation.

The truth about disappointment, whether it's due to a screw-up or not getting what you want, is that you can kick it out anytime you choose. Unlike a headache, which you have to treat with medication or meditation, disappointment doesn't really exist. You've created both the size and scope of what you're feeling, and you can stop those thoughts or reduce them anytime you want.

A CEO told me a line that always works for him, to quickly get over feelings of inadequacy: "It only hurts when you think about it." If you stop thinking about disappointment or humiliation, it won't hurt anymore, or at least you will be able to free up your mind to think about other things.

• **Being a little imperfect is being a lot human.** The intensity of our disappointment always relates to how perfect we think we are. If we build ourselves up as flawless, we will fall hard when flaws emerge.

One way to avoid building yourself up too high is to constantly challenge the image you have of yourself. If you see yourself as perfect, recognize your imperfections. Take responsibility for mistakes, apologize for errors, laugh at yourself, and admit when you need help. The more comfortable you are with your flaws, the less surprised you'll be when mistakes remind you of them.

• **The sooner I get busy, the sooner I'll get over it.** Nothing erases disappointment faster than new challenges. Whatever loss you have suffered, your suffering will be eased if you busy yourself quickly. New challenges and accomplishments serve as expanding distractions that stop obsessive thinking and help you rebuild whatever self-esteem you lost overanalyzing your disappointment.

This isn't to say that you should ignore disappointment or camouflage it with busywork. But once you think through the problem and understand why it happened, you should take steps to occupy your mind with other things. Otherwise, negative thoughts crop up like weeds and you'll begin to put yourself down in an effort to rationalize what happened, especially if there isn't an obvious explanation.

Keeping yourself busy opens your mind and other thoughts rush in, pushing out the old ones. One thought generates two others, and the two create four more, and the next thing you know, the space in your mind that was dominated by disappointment is occupied by questions, challenges, and new dreams.

■ CHAPTER FIFTEEN ■

Watch Your Back

Prosperity makes few friends.

ANONYMOUS

The more fortunate you become, the greater the odds that you'll make people envious of you. It can't be helped. There are always going to be people who wish they had what you possess. But some will become so upset by your good fortune that they will want to see you knocked back down to size and may even be motivated to take steps to undermine and reverse your good fortune.

To limit your bad luck, you have to be aware of the people who are resentful, and take steps to neutralize or avoid them whenever possible. Every so often, it pays to see what's going on behind you. I'm not suggesting that you become preoccupied with people who don't like you or that you become obsessed with destroying your enemies. That would defeat the whole purpose of making good luck happen. You simply want to watch your back, so that attacks from the rear do not come as a surprise and you're prepared to deflect or stop them.

We know that bad luck strikes when we least expect it. What most people don't realize, however, is that much of that bad luck comes because we failed to spot the people who want to begrudge us our achievements and are working against us. It's not about paranoia or seeking revenge. Watching your back is about studying the behavior of people who are close to you, reexamining relationships, and weeding out those who can undermine all of your luck-making efforts. It pays to be just a little suspicious.

You Cause Resentment, You Can Stop It

Everyone has dreams and aspirations. That's why we get out of bed every day. We want to be happy. But different things make different people happy, and there are times when two or more people want the same thing. It may be to date the same guy or girl, win the same job, or buy the same house. There are rules by which we play when competing for those things, such as "first come first serve" or "may the best person win."

But even when we live by those laws, it doesn't mean we're happy about it when the other person wins. That's why your happiness will always trigger feelings of resentment in other people. When you're happy, you're bound to cause someone to want to saw your head off. Temper how you demonstrate your happiness, and you'll limit resentment.

When feelings of resentment are stirred up sufficiently, people will begrudge you your good fortune. No one is immune from this negative feeling, not even friends or relatives. How often do we hear that someone's father is jealous of his son's success? Or that colleagues who work for the same company are at war because one has the ear of higher-ups and the other doesn't? Or that inlaws of lottery winners are suing for a piece of the jackpot?

When someone feels left out, their instinct is to take away or destroy the other person's achievement. If you want to know why, just visit any playground sandbox for ten minutes or so. You'll see one kid with a great toy having fun. Sooner or later another kid comes along and kicks the toy or takes it away. He isn't satisfied until the other kid is no longer happy or is crying. Misery loves company, and this is especially true when your success or happiness makes other people feel unsuccessful or unhappy.

Stop Bitter People from Getting the Better of You

No matter how careful you are to tone down your exuberance when you've capitalized on an opportunity or when life goes your way, people are going to be gritting their teeth. That's the way it goes. You just don't want that resentment to turn into a grudge. Then the amount of luck that comes your way risks being compromised.

Here's how to reduce the odds of that happening . . .

• **Don't showboat when you win.** Professional athletes aren't very good role models. When they score touchdowns, slam-dunk baskets, or sink a putt, they perform rituals that show off their feelings. High-fives, hanging from the rim of a hoop, or hurling a golf club in the air after winning are common images on TV.

If you were to "hang from the rim" at work or brag too much after winning approval for a proposed project, you'd find yourself in deep trouble. Such displays of intense emotion alienate other people and remind them that they have yet to achieve what they want. People will either desert you or wish you bad luck. You want to be happy, but remain with the pack. If you pull too far ahead, they'll want to cut you off.

I remember baseball great Hank Aaron being asked once why pitchers didn't try to hit him with the ball to keep him from blasting a career record 755 home runs. He said that instead of intimidating the pitcher after hitting a homer by standing at home plate, watching the ball sail out of the park, and cockily running the bases, he just humbly ran the bases. As a result, pitchers never tried to block his quest of Babe Ruth's home-run record by trying to hit him or knock him down.

As Hank Aaron knows, most people can go a lot further if they master the art of quiet happiness. True happiness is inner peace, self-satisfaction, and a conviction that you've accomplished something special. If you have to share these feelings, do so in a way that respects others' feelings. Be aware that your happiness will illuminate someone else's failure. Reflect on what you've achieved before you broadcast it, and then find the right tone and volume before you promote your achievements. You need to let people know that you're lucky in order to make more luck. But you should not reveal your pleasure recklessly or use it as a weapon of revenge. This attitude will only create more resentment.

• **Don't try to score over and over again.** I make this mistake all the time. I've always tried to pull off the impossible at work, trying to get people brilliant in their fields to cooperate with my writers. It's a great thrill when they agree. But in my rush to execute everything perfectly, I often forget that you have to let other people shine. Otherwise you trigger hostility, like the athlete who never passes the ball. Even though you're scoring points, you need to give others a chance.

In 1990, when I was hired to be the business editor at *Working Woman*, I was the only male editor at the magazine. I was brought in to add a different tone and insight to articles run in the publication. In the beginning, I was really stupid. I didn't see that my being the only man on staff would cause resentment. I also was blind to the fact that my close relationship with the editor-in-chief would cause a great deal of envy and friction. Within weeks after I started, someone sneaked into the personnel department's file cabinet. My salary was discovered and leaked around the office, compromising my privacy.

Had I to do it over again, I probably would have tried to keep a lower profile and not have been so competitive. It may not have helped, however, since many people on staff were unhappy that I was there to begin with. But a more subtle approach may have reduced the intense level of staff envy and hostility.

• **Bewilderment makes others happy.** One of the best ways to avoid triggering envy is to be dumbfounded by your own good fortune. The more innocent you appear and the less it seems you had anything to do with your success, the less likely you are to arouse envy. You want to be happy, but you don't want your exuberance to put you on other people's screens. Fly low so that you escape detection and keep others from going on the offensive to upset your lucky streak.

Remarking that you don't know how your good fortune happened or that it's all a great big surprise to you puts others at ease. Shrug your shoulders, and people will leave you alone. But throw your fists up in the air, and people will want you to experience a big loss to even the score.

• **Feel a little miserable.** Another way to avoid making people envious is to express misery before they take steps to make you miserable. Too much joy attracts people who want you to experience a little pain and sorrow. But if you express your unhappiness a little, you will have beaten them to it. I know a lucky person who from time to time tells people that things aren't going well just to offset her lucky image.

Expressing disappointment lets people know that life doesn't always go your way. Even your mild unhappiness will make others feel better about themselves and keep them from wishing you harm. In fact, if you do it right, they'll feel a little sorry for you and leave you alone. By throwing your potential adversaries a bone, you can keep them away from your leg.

• **Hide your booty.** Don't flaunt what you've achieved or brag about what you've accomplished. You're better off camouflaging your great achievements rather than strutting around with them high over your head. Showing off a new sports car, a new office, or anything else that other people will wish they had is a dangerous gambit. Let people discover the good things that you've come into rather than displaying them too openly.

Modesty and privacy are the best firewalls between you and bad luck. My rule of thumb is simple: Share good news with your friends and bad news with your enemies, and you'll never be ambushed.

How to Neutralize a Stalker

Despite your best efforts, there are going to be people who will want to chop you down to size. They will want you to experience bad luck or share their suffering. Unless you neutralize these people, they eventually will succeed.

Here are a few strategies that lucky people use when people have already begun taking steps to upend them . . .

• **Spend a little time with hostile people so they think your luck might rub off on them.** People who are most envious of you simply want you to pay attention to them. While you should avoid negative people at all costs, sometimes they can't be sidestepped. When this happens, your best bet is to pay attention to them, if only for a little while. Lunch with them, meet with them, talk on the phone with them, and acknowledge them. They will feel more comfortable with you, and they may come to believe that you perhaps deserve what you have achieved.

• **Make a little luck for them.** If you can't beat them, give them a piece of what you've achieved. I know someone who was promoted to a high position. She was given a great office and use of a car service to go home each night. These perks caused a great deal of envy among two other people at the office—that is, until she began ferrying her adversaries home each night. Despite their envy, they couldn't say no to the convenience of getting a lift home. Their only option was the subway or paying for a cab themselves.

This woman made her colleagues feel lucky, which helped them feel better about her success. After a while, the rides home stopped coming as frequently, since the woman had business obligations or wasn't around as often. But because she had shared her good luck, the negative feelings among her former rivals weren't as pointed. Eventually, they accepted the woman's promotion.

• **Stay away from them entirely, and hope for the best.** Sometimes throwing envious people a bone doesn't work, nor does much of anything else. Whenever you score, there are going to be people who are impossible to placate. They aren't going to be happy until they've made your life miserable.

The best way to keep this from happening is to stay away from these people entirely. If you do not talk to them or interact with them, they won't be part of your world and probably won't care whether you have good luck or not. Remember, people become envious only when they feel on equal footing with you and are exposed to your good fortune. If you dodge them, you are no longer part of their universe and therefore your triumphs have nothing to do with them.

If you can't help but be associated with extremely envious people, either because you work with them or are friends with people who are friendly with them, do everything you can to quarantine them. Embargo all news about yourself or resist getting into much detail when you share information about yourself. The less you interact with them, the less likely it is that they will create bad luck for you.

Beware of Backstabbers

I know it sounds paranoid, but pushed the wrong way, there are some people out there who are just waiting to blindside you with a little bad luck. Everyone has adversaries, and the luckier you become, the more these adversaries are going to try to sneak up behind you and shove you off course.

Sometimes these backstabbers act quickly. Sometimes it takes years for them to make their move. Some of them deliver lots of little stabs over long periods of time while others get it all out of their system with one thrust. Whatever the case, their prime mission is to assassinate your character.

"I know that there are always going to be people who will try to run me down," says a prominent executive I know. "And I don't care. I just want to know who the people are before they do too much damage. I'm not interested in hurting them or punishing them. That would use up too much of the energy I need to make things happen. I just want to keep them at arm's length. Otherwise, they could do real damage to my reputation."

Keeping these people at arm's length sometimes means not letting them know that you are aware of their negative intentions. In some cases, it may mean you should modify your relationship with them. In other cases, it means getting rid of them as friends or colleagues. But in every case, you need to spot the signs of people who want to see you fail.

"I divide everyone into supporters and saboteurs," says my executive friend. "Supporters help me and are genuine friends. They are there when I need them, and they want me to do well. It takes time for these people to prove themselves through their actions. Saboteurs are the people who look for an opening in order to give me a shot. For years, I used to overlook the saboteurs in my life, sort of laughing off their indiscretions and bad judgment. I assumed I was above them. But these people can really hurt you unless you keep them at a safe distance."

In some respects, distance is exactly what saboteurs want. They don't really want to hurt or destroy you, only to keep you from making them feel inferior. If they can rattle your nerves just enough, they figure you'll lose your edge and some of your good luck. In many cases, you don't have to abandon these people completely.

"I had this friend some years ago with whom I was very, very close," my friend says. "We would be together all of the time, at work, at lunch, after work, and sometimes on the weekend. But over time, my luck improved and hers didn't. That's when our friendship began to turn into something else. I guess familiarity does breed contempt. I really liked her, but I backed off a little. We stopped lunching so often, and we stopped socializing after work. It was perfect, because it allowed us to develop a different type of friendship. The intensity of our previous relationship, when I was doing well and she was not, actually was turning her into the kind of nasty person she really wasn't. My success was eating her up, especially in contrast with her own bad luck.

"By pulling back and quietly redrawing the lines of the relationship, both of us had some breathing room. It restored her dignity. We remain friends to this day, but by recognizing her character flaw and seeing that she was capable of taking certain liberties that could hurt me, I changed the dynamics. I knew she didn't mean the things she did. To this day she probably doesn't even realize what she did. But by pulling back, I'm able to have her as a friend without letting her get close enough to do me harm."

Like my executive friend, there may come a point when your success becomes too much for an acquaintance or colleague of yours to hear. Unless you are cognizant of the pain that your growth and gains are having on this person, you may find yourself caught between loyalty and liability.

True friends usually feel great when good things happen to you. They want to celebrate, they want you to know how much they support you, and they will do anything to help you get what you want. They don't begrudge you your good fortune. But sometimes friendships become strained when you become luckier.

Even friends need to know what they can and can't do. They need to know that in order to remain friendly with you, the same basic rules of friendship—respect, trust, kindness—apply as before you became "lucky." If your friend can't handle your good fortune, perhaps you need to take a break from each other.

How to Protect Your Back

Now that you know why even the people you consider friends do crazy things when your luck improves, you'll want to take steps to protect yourself as you become luckier. You want to be made aware of someone's indiscretion before they know you know. Like good card players, you need to have a good indication of what other people are holding so that you can play your cards to win.

Here are the strategies shrewd people
use to protect their backs . . .

• **Set up a network of supporters.** These aren't necessarily your

friends, though they can be. They are what one person I know calls
"sentries." Like the guards at a fort, they are loyal and highly obser-
vant. They can alert you to bad luck that's headed your way. There
have been several times in my own career when people have let me
know when there was a problem I had to solve. The advance warning allowed me to straighten out the situation before it turned into
"bad luck." To encourage such well-placed people to keep you well-
informed, you need only ask them.

You want to encourage them to report back to you, but you also
want to be mindful of the information they bring back. Never act
immediately on the information you receive, because you never know
how accurate or pure it is—even if the information comes from someone you trust. Everyone puts a spin on things. Sometimes they embel-
lish a little to make themselves look good.

Be especially wary when someone tells you that someone else is
"out to get you." That line is so destructive and is probably responsible
for ruining more relationships than any other single phrase. When
you are told that someone is out to get you, even if you can't verify the
truth of the warning, your first reaction may be to retaliate against that
individual the messenger is talking about. Even if you later discover
that this person isn't out to get you, you'll likely have trouble really
trusting that person again.

So when people tell you someone is gunning for you, always let the
information sit for a while. Keep an eye on the situation, but always
assume it's completely false. You don't want to wait until you're under
attack. But you also don't want to go on the offensive based on
hearsay, even when it comes from a trusted source. Remember, information can be conveyed dozens of different ways. You have to ask
yourself why the person who gave you this information is presenting it
that way before you act based on what they've told you.

• **Set a trust trap.** Some people I know actually test out their sentries. Their argument is that they have to know whom they can trust and whom they can't. Trust is the key. Some people are great friends but can't keep from gossiping with others and sharing information you both agreed was confidential. Other people keep what you tell them a secret and never violate that trust. How can you determine whom you can trust with information and whom you cannot?

One interesting strategy someone told me about is a "trust trap." Tell your "sentry" something inconsequential, but be sure to emphasize that what you're saying is in strict confidence. Then if what you've said gets around, you'll know the person can't be trusted. You need to set these types of traps for people, this person said, because it's the only way to size up their motives and agendas. In the final analysis, the only people worth trusting are those who can keep a secret.

Another test you can give is the "truth test." Find out what happened first, and then ask someone else to tell you what happened. This will let you know how greatly this person exaggerates the truth. Again, this is not a test to determine which of your friends to keep and which to discard. It's simply a way to assess the quality of the information that you receive and limit your bad luck by identifying the people who can hurt you.

■ CHAPTER SIXTEEN ■

Bad Luck Is Good Luck

Don't be afraid to fail. A lot of people have to fail to be successful.
A lot of people on top have had bad things happen to them.

MICHAEL JORDAN

Despite your best efforts, you are going to experience bad luck. There's nothing you can do about it. Your interactions with random events will inevitably result in setbacks. All you can do is hope that your misfortunes aren't too serious and that you can put them behind you as soon as possible.

When we experience bad luck, whether it is random or self-created, we become different people—weak, depressed, or angry. Bad luck is terrifying. It makes us stop thinking about the future's possibilities. It makes us feel cursed and doomed to spend eternity living an existence that keeps getting worse.

One reason we feel this way is that we aren't sure how long our bad luck is going to last or whether more bad luck is on its way. While you can't completely avoid bad luck, you can cut down on the amount you experience if you manage your crises well. Lucky people tend to position misfortune in a way that doesn't invite negative attention. Whatever problems they experience, they project an image and outlook that puts other people at ease. They view misfortune not as a dead end or as a warning to give up, but as a pause along the way to realizing their dreams. Rather than fold up, they force themselves to embrace bad luck and see it as a rich learning experience.

Only then can they find the "secret passage" that exists in every seemingly bad situation. This secret passage is some opportunity that will allow you to escape your terrible predicament. The trick is to look for this secret passage rather than assume you must live under the oppressive weight of your misfortune.

Bad luck helps you develop survival instincts and skills that you didn't have before. It also forces you to experiment, leading you to discover aspects of yourself that you never knew existed. But to view misfortune as an opportunity, you must first believe that you are eventually going to succeed.

We All React to Bad Luck Differently

The first thought that may cross your mind when bad luck strikes is, "Why me?" Bad luck makes us feel helpless. We're unsure what is going to happen to us. We're dazed, confused, and upset. We all pride ourselves on being in control of our lives, and we all like to think we're doing a great job of making life work in our favor. Misfortune sends us into an emotional tailspin because it contradicts the image we have of ourselves as successful and competent.

How long you're down emotionally depends on how badly you were hit. What you tend to forget during this traumatic experience is that people are watching to see how you'll weather the storm. Some of these people are going to be glad that you are in trouble, because they feel that you deserve it. But the people who count most in your life—

the ones with the golden opportunities—are going to be rooting for you. They will be watching to see how quickly you can get back on track. Your reputation is on the line when bad luck strikes and others become aware of your troubles. How you handle yourself will mean the difference between getting people to help you and being ignored.

Some people handle misfortune well. They are stunned by the experience but quickly take steps to manage a crisis. They keep their troubles to themselves, or they go out of their way to explain their bad luck in a way that makes people want to help them rather than run the other way. If you can demonstrate that you're a fighter and that misfortune doesn't bother you too much, people will want to assist you. That's because others will realize that you probably won't need too much help and you aren't likely to bring misfortune on them. But if you appear to be a clinger—someone who lunges at other people and desperately clings to them for aid—don't expect much assistance. You'll seem like someone about to drown, and others will be afraid that you'll drag them down with you.

So how you react personally and publicly to misfortune determines whether or not people will help you and whether you will have more bad luck or turn bad luck to good.

Put a Positive Spin on Bad News

The more mindful you are that your image and reputation have a direct impact on your luck, the more likely you are to take steps to protect them, especially in a crisis.

Putting a "spin" on bad news may sound like deception, but it's not. Spin is the way in which negative news is related so that the people involved look less bad than they have to. Every story can be told a dozen different ways and still be accurate and truthful. Spin is merely adding point of view to the facts to minimize or maximize particular aspects of those facts. There's nothing wrong with spin, except when it results in a lie. We all take the facts and tell them in a particular order to blunt the pain or to pump up what we want to highlight. Spin is important because it creates lasting impressions. When it's done right, people understand the facts—and see them from the perspective you want them to have.

Here's how lucky people position bad luck
to make themselves look good . . .

• **Give the bad news first.** Most people report bad news in a way that makes the news sound worse than it is. Their mistake is that they report the bad news second, not first. They try to soften up the listener by setting up the bad news with lighter information: "A few things happened today. Let me tell you about something funny that happened first . . ." Or they try to prepare the listener by hinting that they are about to deliver bad news: "Before you get angry, I just wanted to say that there wasn't much we could do about what happened . . ."

Many people think this strategy will ease the sting. Unfortunately, this strategy is highly undesirable and will always make the news and you look worse, not better. By trying to sweeten or delay your bad news, you inadvertently cause the listener either to become too relaxed or to tense up in anticipation of bad news.

Yet, when we're doing the listening, we like bad news up-front and fast. When we're doing the telling, we think it's smart to sugar-coat bad news. Bad news is usually not as bad as you think it is. It only seems that way.

"When I have something bad to relate that involves me, I consciously run through several opening lines that place the bad news in the first sentence that comes out of my mouth," says an advertising executive who knows a thing or two about spin. "Giving them the bad news first gets it out of the way. But it does more, psychologically. Delivering the bad news up-front is like accidentally setting a fire that you then help to put out. Your help is what's remembered, not the fact that you might be an arsonist.

"A few weeks ago my group at the agency lost some business from a sportswear company. I headed up the account, so I had to break the news to the head of the department here. When she picked up the phone, I said, 'Hi, it's Joe. Listen, we lost the sportswear business. I feel terrible, but I have a good idea what we did wrong, and I know what we can do to make sure it doesn't happen again. Can I come by and talk to you about it?'

"By positioning bad news this way, the focus was on the solution, not the problem or the fact that I was delivering it. When I saw my boss, she wanted to know why exactly we lost the business and all of the other details. I was no longer the problem but the problem-solver. Getting her involved with the solution made her part of the team rather than the overseer. Everything worked out."

By coming right out with bad news, you come across as someone who is honest and unafraid of bad luck.

• **Compare bad news to worse news.** There are times when your bad news is so problematic that you have to tell even worse news first to put it in a more favorable light.

To pull off this approach effectively, you have to shock the other person first with terrible news and then slip in your bad news afterward. "It's like the story about the girl who writes home from college to her parents," says an investment banker I know. "'Dear Mom and Dad,' she writes, 'It's been so long since I've written but the prisons don't let you write that often. I was arrested for robbing a bank with my boyfriend. I haven't told you about him because he's not the same religion we are and he lives in a dangerous neighborhood. We've both been sick for months, but I'm afraid to seek medical attention. Oh, by the way, there is no jail, no boyfriend, no bank robbery, and no illness. I got a C in chemistry, and I could use one hundred dollars until the holidays.' The bad news sounds great by comparison. All is forgiven, and the girl gets her money.

"Many mutual funds do this all the time. Instead of telling potential investors that their expenses are high, they first tell them that the expenses of the industry's average fund are higher. Then they tell them that their funds' expenses are lower. Forget about the fact that the fund is charging a rate that's higher than many other funds. By comparing the fund's rate with the industry average, the fund's rate seems low."

• **Tell the truth.** For you to look good when you look bad, you must have integrity. Leaving out information is always better than telling a lie, because the truth has a funny way of coming out eventually. When you're caught in a lie, you can kiss your good luck good-bye. Lies are rarely forgiven or forgettable. Most people can take hearing the truth. What they can't take and won't forgive easily is dishonesty. So give the other person the information he or she needs to know, and move on. Honesty is a great way to look good in a bad situation. Because everyone recognizes that it's hard to be honest, you will be admired.

"I recently needed brochures designed for my business," says a friend who runs a catering company. "The first designer I used was late with the job. Rather than giving me advance warning, she told me a day after the job was due that she needed more time. Then she was late again, this time blaming the delay on her paper supplier. I fired her. The next designer I used was late with her work too, but she told me a week in advance that she had run into trouble. She gave me a second date and was on time. Now she's doing an even bigger job for us. Both designers screwed up, but the second one told me the bad news immediately. She was honest about it. I felt bad for her, but not bad about her."

When you're honest about your difficulties, you become sympathetic and attract luck because people can relate to your problems. Hide the truth and people think you're shifty and unreliable.

• **Don't complain.** One of the most interesting articles I have read on attracting luck appeared recently in the Sunday *New York Times*. It was headlined "He's Getting By with a Little Help from His Friends." The article was about a teenage boy from Maine whose depressed father had tried to commit suicide and whose mother was committed to a mental institution. The teen was left on his own and was clearly someone most people would have stayed away from, given all of his emotional baggage.

Yet his best friend's family took him in, and the family of the boy's girlfriend helped too. Why? According to the people quoted in the article, the teen was extremely likable. He didn't complain, he wasn't a burden, he had nice manners, and rarely asked for help. He knew how to blend in. "If you look at him, you don't see a kid who seems to come from the depths of poverty," said the father of the teen's best friend. "He keeps himself clean, dresses well, knows how to get along with people and what he needs."

Despite the teen's terrible misfortunes, he limited how much more bad luck his situation was going to produce by counteracting misfortune with behavior that made him irresistible. As corny as it sounds, bad-luck streaks can sometimes be stopped if you do nothing more than put on a happy face and stop worrying about your troubles. At the very least, you will attract help, which will replace your bad luck little by little.

When Bad Luck Strikes, Go to the Movies

Some people go through life from crisis to crisis. They spend most of their energy struggling to emerge from setbacks. Their greatest desire is that the crisis they're dealing with at any given moment will end, and that a small pocket of tranquillity will exist before the next unexpected crisis hits.

Lucky people view life and themselves differently. Their outlook is much more panoramic. They look for the opportunity in every setback and aren't petrified by bad luck, nor do they see every misfortune in cataclysmic terms. They shift their thinking about achieving what they want from "maybe" to "when." Such thinking requires a very special outlook on life and the role you play in it.

Many lucky people who minimize misfortune carry around in their minds a heroic image of themselves. They create a self-impression that is so strong that it serves as a motivation and a self-defense mechanism whenever tough times and discouragement set in. These images are packaged like a "coming attraction" at the movies.

In this so-called mini-movie, you are the star who, in the end, achieves what you set out to accomplish, despite all of the obstacles you face along the way. Your mental movie should be like any epic or love story, in which the hero or heroine has ups and downs but in the end is victorious. Setbacks are nothing more than events to be brushed aside, not reasons to give up. "Film," or imagine, yourself winding up happy, rich, or working at a job you love.

The more vivid the images you have of yourself succeeding, the faster you will trick your mind into believing you're going to overcome setbacks and get what you want. Your mind will become activated, and opportunities that can help you, even in a crisis, will start flashing. When you experience bad luck, run this reel in your mind and it will magically restore your conviction and recharge your energy and enthusiasm.

How to film a lucky "mind movie" of yourself . . .

• **Spend an hour or so thinking of yourself as the hero or heroine of an adventure movie or drama.** Imagine you are in all the major scenes. You're the one everyone in the movie looks up to and depends on.

• **Write the mental screenplay**. Start with the ending: You win and get what you want. Then work your way backward. You're on a noble quest, a voyage. You are going to meet evil forces along the way that will try to prevent you from reaching your goal.

• **In the movie, you battle life's negative forces but are always up to the challenge.** Some battles last longer than others, but you will triumph in the end because you are determined to reach your goal at all costs.

• **Visualize a grand finale in which a major battle rages or an enormous challenge arises.** You fight hard and win. The movie music swells, you're a hero, and the credits come up.

Visualizing yourself in these terms may seem silly, but it will have an immediate impact on how you think about good luck and bad luck. Consider your happiness as an all-important quest and something to which you are entitled. This image will help you to spend most of your time finding ways to make good luck happen even when you experience misfortune.

Bad Luck Leads to Good Luck, Eventually

Ironically, it is often your bad-luck experiences that lead to much of your good luck. Hardship breeds inner strength and new ways of coping. It also pushes you to develop new ways of solving problems. To start seeing hardship from this perspective, you must stop believing that setbacks can be forever eliminated. Life doesn't work this way. When you think it does, bad luck becomes much more traumatic and debilitating because it is that much more unexpected. If you anticipate bad luck, you won't be so surprised when it strikes. Instead, you will begin to build yourself up and look for the opportunities that exist in bad luck's shadows.

"My luckiest clients are a couple who one day in the 1980s found themselves with no source of income," says money manager Michael Stolper. "He was an air-traffic controller who was fired when President Reagan refused to give in to strikers' demands. She was a housewife. They couldn't find work and were eating peanut butter and jelly sandwiches and cereal at every meal just to survive. Then they began to enter the contests mentioned on the backs of the cereal boxes. They had so much fun doing that, they started a newsletter that reported on all of the contests and how readers could improve their odds of winning. The newsletter was written in a very kitchen-table style, so it was incredibly appealing. The newsletter became so big that they eventually sold it for about $8 million. Today, their life is defined by their hiking trips and the number of Ritz-Carltons they stay in."

Falling upward. It's the ultimate good luck experience. A terrible misfortune leaves you on the brink of disaster only to be followed by success beyond your wildest dreams. We like to believe that people who experienced amazing turnarounds were innocent bystanders. But in most cases they weren't. I know several superlucky people who have suffered tremendous setbacks only to wind up successful a short time later. They all have several things in common.

For starters, all superlucky people believe that today's disaster is temporary, not permanent. They also rarely put themselves down or feel ashamed when they experience bad luck. Instead, they believe their bad luck isn't personal and will disappear if they forget about it and move on. Some superlucky people don't even care whether other people think they're losers or fools. So much the better, because the more oblivious and nonchalant these superlucky people seem about their misfortune, the more people are willing to throw them a few scraps of opportunity. People who fall up believe that much of what we think of as bad luck actually is nothing more than the shock of disappointment compounded by the sting of rejection.

Unfortunately, not enough people think lucky, and when bad luck strikes, they lack the skills to transform misfortune into good luck. Being told that we aren't valuable is traumatic, and our nightmares can be much more vivid than our dreams. We hope for the best but often imagine the worst. We hope that our talents will be discovered and rewarded handsomely, but too few of us believe this miracle will really happen. Most of us assume that it is the other guy's setbacks that lead to triumphs, not ours.

I have come to believe that bad things happen for good reasons. I've had my share of disappointment and rejection. But I've found that in every case I was lucky to have lost the opportunity that I thought was ideal, because a subsequent opportunity turned out to be a blessing.

There was the time I was up for the media critic's job at *U.S. News & World Report* in Washington, D.C. I had worked with one of the magazine's managing editors when he was at the *New York Times,* and he set up an interview for me with one of his top editors. I blew the interview by foolishly taking an antihistamine a few hours before my meeting and wound up answering questions in slow motion. But had I gotten the job, the woman I had just started dating in New York City would not have commuted and probably would have ended the relationship. I stayed in New York, and she became my wife.

Then there was a big interview with the CEO of a major media company in New York. I was prepared for the meeting, but it was the only time in my life that I forgot to double-check the location the day before. The company has two main offices, and I wound up at the wrong one—two miles away and five minutes to go before my meeting. A sympathetic cab driver took chase-scene chances in midtown traffic, and I arrived only ten minutes late. But my clothes and hair were a mess after racing through the summer morning heat. I was off-balance in my interview and played defensive rather than setting the tone. I didn't get the job, but a month later I was given a big promotion and raise at the publication where I worked at the time.

I even had an interview set up with a top executive from a top entertainment company who never showed up for breakfast, despite the fact that he had called the meeting. Instead, he hired one of my friends. Six months later, the executive was fired—and so was my friend, who calls me every so often for freelance work.

Life plays funny tricks on you—and the more the merrier, I say. I always assume that the bad things that happen to me happen for a reason, and I try to fall upward as often as possible. To keep my sense of perspective, I remind myself that somewhere out there somebody has it much worse than I do. No matter how hard life seems, I never forget how lucky I am.

One of the best pieces of advice I ever received was from a friend I worked with some years ago who was fired from a job as a magazine editor and then became rich after writing a book that became a huge bestseller. When I asked whether her getting fired made her doubt whether she'd ever get what she wanted in life, she said, "Sure—for about a day. But I've come to learn that bad luck is nothing more than good luck with a chip on its shoulder."

About the Author

Marc Myers is executive editor and editor-in-chief, respectively, of *Bottom Line/Personal* and *Moneysworth,* two of the country's largest and best-known "how-to" consumer newsletters. He has appeared on NBC's *Today* show, ABC's *Nightline* and on CNN, where he appeared in a live weekly segment. His articles have appeared in the *New York*  *Times, Parents, McCall's, Working Woman,* and *Adweek,* on a variety of topics, including self-help, career, and the sexes. He has spoken publicly on luck and the workplace, most recently at the annual meeting of International Executive Recruiters at New York's Grand Hyatt Hotel. At *Bottom Line/Personal* and *Moneysworth,* he has edited and has developed relationships with such well-known people as M. Scott Peck, Stephen Covey, Wayne Dyer, Tony Robbins, Olivia Goldsmith, Bernie Siegel, Nathaniel Branden, Dean Ornish, Mark Victor Hansen, Jack Canfield, Deepak Chopra, Andrew Weil, and many other best-selling self-improvement authors. He lives in New York City with his wife and daughter.

PHOTO BY WENDY BARROWS